The On-Your-Own Cookbook

June Roth

The On-Your-Own Cookbook

*How to
Cope in the Kitchen*

The Dial Press • New York • 1972

Library of Congress Cataloging in Publication Data

Roth, June Spiewak.
    The on-your-own cookbook.

    1. Cookery.   I. Title.
TX715.R842   641.5   75–37465

To my nieces and nephews,
with much love aforethought

Contents

Dear Reader,

*Who cares whether you take the time to prepare yourself an appetizing meal?
I do! And that's why I have taken the time to write a book just for you who
are on your own.*

*There is a difference between feeding and dining, and I hope you like
yourself well enough to experience the pleasure of a well-planned meal. These
recipes were devised for busy people who may be new to the kitchen . . . taking
into consideration your small amount of time to spend, your probable lack of
knowledge and equipment, and your desire for food that looks as though you
are a gourmet cook. All the recipes are easy to prepare and have a certain flair
that will make you feel your efforts are worthwhile.*

*Food preparation can be a creative art form that challenges your individu-
ality and gives satisfaction to your palate. It pleases me to think that I may
play a small part in helping you to cope with being on your own.*

Sincerely,
JUNE ROTH

1 · Gracious Survival

If home is a great place to visit, but you don't want to live there—it's time to learn a few things about gracious survival. For one of the pitfalls of being on your own is having to cope with that old habit called "eating."

You can stave off panic temporarily by using TV dinners or opening a can of tuna. You can feed at the local diner or buy expensive and dreary delicatessen. And perhaps you can wangle enough invitations to postpone elementary education in the kitchen. But eventually you will want to learn a few tricks such as:

WHAT TO DO: To keep your kitchen organized.

WHAT TO BUY: So you won't fade out from malnutrition!

HOW TO BUY IT: So you won't waste your tightly budgeted food money on poor selections.

HOW TO STORE IT: So you won't chance ptomaine and other spoilage problems that can turn good food into garbage before its time.

HOW TO COOK IT: So you can continue the habit of dining with pleasure.

HOW TO STRETCH IT: So you can get the most mileage out of your cooking efforts and your food dollars.

Half the fun of being on your own is eating and entertaining at your own pace to suit your life-style of the moment. Knowing that you have a busy life, I aim here to condense the knowledge and techniques that experienced cooks take for granted. A vocabulary chapter has been included, in case a recipe has a direction that you do not understand. Refer to the vocabulary as you would a foreign language list, and you will soon begin to understand cooking and function in the kitchen with expertise.

Most of the recipes have been designed to serve two or three people, but directions are also included for serving four to six. This will enable you to cook for a roommate or husband—or to cook for two days' time if you are alone—yet confidently expand the recipes to serve several guests. Larger-quantity recipes have also been included for those times when you plan to entertain a larger group. Shortcuts are given whenever possible, although many start-from-scratch recipes have been included for your gourmet moods.

A special chapter tells you how to get a party started, with recipes for dips and spreadables that will help you to entertain nicely even if you're on a budget.

To get the most use from this book, sit down first and read it through as you would a long letter from someone who cares. Then place the book in your kitchen for easy reference and browse through it from time to time to jog your appetite and inspire yourself to try something new.

At first, cooking may seem too difficult for you to master, but if you will think back to when you learned to drive a car, you'll remember that the rules and equipment seemed overwhelming then, too. This time, there's no license to be won and you have a lifetime ahead in which to practice. The only test will be in the tasting, and all accidents can be salvaged or disposed of without guilt. Just keep in mind that knowledge is your best insurance policy and a little freewheeling always makes cooking more fun.

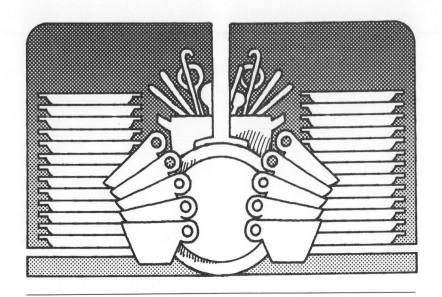

2 · Kitchen Engineering

Most new cooks get bogged down when cleaning up their kitchens. Cooking itself is an art form that gives emotional as well as gustatorial satisfaction, but anyone who says that cleaning up a pile of dirty dishes is fun must be joking. The trick is to prevent a pileup of work whenever you can.

Never—just never—put dirty dishes, bowls, and utensils in a heap in the sink and figure that you'll do them later! Before you start to cook, fill a basin with hot water and detergent and place it in the sink. Put a rack on the drainboard. Place a dish towel next to it. Now you are ready to prepare your meal, and as you finish with a dish, bowl, or utensil—dunk it, rinse it, and put it in the drainer. If you need it again, fish it out clean from the drainer. If not, dry it and put it away while the range does the cooking and you're just watching.

Use the same trick during dinner, especially if you are serving company, and you will find that as you are having dessert most of the dishes will be out of the sink and almost dry enough to put away.

No pileup and no trying to scrub dried food from resistant kitchenware hours later! This works with pots and pans too—never let them sit with sticky residues of food without at least pouring hot water and a squirt of detergent in them. Keep a half yard of nylon netting near the sink—fold it up into a pad and run the pad around the soiled pans. It will pick up all excess food and stickiness, and rinse out into a fast-drying, multi-use rag.

You may go through a phase of being "kitchen-gadget happy" and begin to acquire every potential time-saver from an electric can opener to a fancy nut grinder. If space and money don't matter to you at all, go ahead and enjoy yourself. But if they are both at a premium, stop and question each purchase as to its usability and necessity in your kitchen. You might be better off spending the money for an electric blender and using a plain can opener that takes about the same amount of time and only a little more wrist motion than its electric counterpart. Once you have decided to buy a kitchen helper, be sure to store it where it will be easy to use. If it's electric, try to locate it on a counter or open shelf. If it's a small hand gadget that you plan to use often, hang it over your work space or put it in one drawer reserved for all your cooking tools. A small piece of pegboard hung near your work area can hold a multitude of quickly grasped items—it keeps them in sight yet neatly out of your way when not in use. If neither a drawer nor pegboard is available for hanging small items, gather all together in a deep mug on your counter—and watch your fingers as you select one from the bouquet.

Here are some kitchen tools that will make your cooking easier; they are worth your investigation and investment:
    Electric blender
    Electric beater (hand variety if you don't intend to bake)
    Electric meat grinder (you may decide you want to grind your
        own meat)
    Several sizes of knives
    Metal whisk (to get omelets, sauces, and soups really smooth)
    Wooden spoons (for stirring without scratching your pots)
    Rubber scraper (to get the last drops that cling to the bowl)
    Can opener
    Vegetable peeler
    Food chopper

Tongs
Ice cream scoop
Measuring cups and spoons
Cooking utensils, including slotted spoon, pancake turner, soup ladle, long fork, and spatula
Colander or strainer

Keep all directions and warranties that accompany your electric equipment so you can refer to them quickly if you have a question about use or care of these products. Pay careful attention to whether electric coffee makers, fry pans, corn poppers, and what-have-you are immersible in water or whether they must be handled gently and rinsed without wetting the mechanisms. Try to clean these things immediately after use so they will stay in good condition for a long time to come.

A sheet of aluminum foil slipped under the broiling rack with the edges squared upward will catch all or most of the drippings as you broil your meats. When this fat solidifies, it is a simple matter to toss out the foil-wrapped drippings and wash the pan in sudsy water. This maneuver saves you from the temptation to spill the fat down the sink drain—a definite "no-no" if you want trouble-free pipes.

If your kitchen isn't arranged so that you can reach for cooking gear at the point of first use, try to rearrange things so you can. You'll save time and motion whenever you prepare a meal if you can get things out quickly.

Cabinets will be of greatest help if you get in the habit of grouping similar kinds of foods together. All mixes, cereals, pasta, and dried foods should be kept in the coolest cabinet you have— that means definitely not over or near the range. Heat brings out a rash of "weevils" in flour products. If you see tiny black dots that move, you have a case of weevils. Check everything in that cabinet, carefully throw out anything in which you find them, wash the cabinet out, and start again. Next time, try to keep all flour items in large jars with tight lids.

It's easier to find a particular can of soup or vegetables if all these cans are always located together. Your refrigerator will be easier to manage, too, if you get in the habit of placing leftovers on one shelf, dairy products on another, and all fruit and vegetables in bins. Place vegetables in plastic bags or wrap them in paper toweling, then place them in the crisper bins in your refrigerator. Line the bins with paper toweling too, and you'll be able to keep them fresh and clean at all times by changing the paper as it gets soiled.

Have a small see-through plastic bin just for cheese. If you keep several kinds of cheese opened at all times, tuck into the bin a folded piece of paper toweling that you have saturated with half vinegar-half water. It will keep the cheese fresh and prevent odors from escaping to other parts of the refrigerator.

Try to keep your dishes in the cabinet nearest to where you dry them. Place the dishes you use most often on the lowest shelf and those you use less often on the upper shelves. Keep your table utensils in the drawer nearest your dining area table. Follow suit with all other items in your kitchen, always trying to locate them near the area where they will be used first. Don't store glasses across the room from the sink—store them right next to the sink, preferably on the side nearest the refrigerator. Place your pots near your range, and your spices on a rack nearby. If you do this kind of grouping, you will find things faster and have less spoilage. One glance in the right direction will tell you the score!

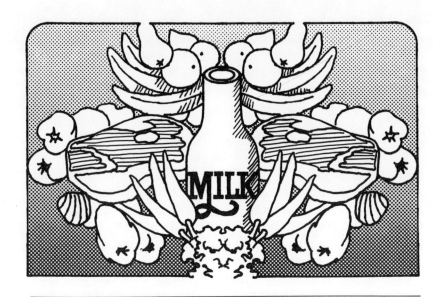

3 · How to Maneuver with Menus

At times, juggling a food budget and achieving balanced nutrition may leave you feeling that you have literally bitten off more than you can chew. Menu planning becomes easier when you have a definite list of "musts" to include for good nutrition. These "musts" fall into four groups:

THE MEAT GROUP
THE MILK GROUP
THE VEGETABLE-FRUIT GROUP
THE BREAD-CEREAL GROUP

Select your daily food servings in the following way:

THE MEAT GROUP: Eat two or more servings a day of meat, poultry, fish, eggs, dry beans, dry peas, lentils, or peanut butter. Each of the following is considered to be one serving:

2 to 3 ounces of boneless meat, poultry, or fish
2 eggs
1 cup cooked dry beans, dry peas, or lentils
4 tablespoons peanut butter

THE MILK GROUP: Eat two or more 8-ounce servings of milk a day. Part or all of the milk may be skim milk, buttermilk, evaporated milk, or dry milk. Substitutions for milk may be made as follows:

1-inch wedge Cheddar cheese equals ½ cup milk or 4 ounces
½ cup cottage cheese equals ⅓ cup milk or 3 ounces
2 tablespoons cream cheese equals 1 tablespoon milk
½ cup ice cream equals ¼ cup milk or 2 ounces

THE VEGETABLE-FRUIT GROUP: Eat four or more servings a day of a variety of fruits and vegetables.

Choose one serving of fruit or vegetable from the Vitamin A list at least every other day. Notice that these foods are all dark green or dark yellow in color; this will help you to remember them.

Choose one serving of citrus fruit or juice from the Vitamin C list every day, and one serving of vegetables from the Vitamin C list every day.

Choose the remaining servings from your own choice of fruits and vegetables or extra servings from the lists that follow.

Vitamin A fruits: apricots, cantaloupe, mango, persimmon

Vitamin A vegetables: broccoli, carrots, chard, collards, cress, kale, pumpkin, spinach, sweet potatoes, turnip greens, winter squash

Vitamin C fruits: grapefruit, guava, honeydew melon, lemon, mango, orange, papaya, strawberries, tangerine, watermelon

Vitamin C vegetables: asparagus, broccoli, brussels sprouts, cabbage, collards, cress, green pepper, kale, kohlrabi, mustard greens, potatoes and sweet potatoes cooked in jackets, spinach, sweet red peppers, tomatoes, turnip greens

THE BREAD-CEREAL GROUP: Eat four or more servings a day. Each of the following is considered to be one serving:

1 slice bread
1 ounce ready-to-eat cereal
½ cup cooked cereal, cornmeal, grits, macaroni, noodles, rice, or spaghetti.

This is the way your "daily dozen" adds up:

2 servings of Meat Group
2 servings of Milk Group
4 servings of Vegetable-Fruit Group
4 servings of Bread-Cereal Group

= *Daily Dozen for Good Health*

Additional food energy and other food values can be obtained from foods that are not in these four food groups. These include all varieties of fats and sweets. Extra servings of the four food groups will be helpful to maintain good nutrition.

With this information as your guide, try to plan your menus for at least three days at a time. Daily food marketing can wreck a budget, for you will be tempted to buy superfluous items, and spur-of-the-moment meals will prevent you from planning good nutrition. Marketing on a twice-weekly basis gives you control over beginning-of-the-week and weekend meals, and it gives you a chance to plan for deliberate leftovers and economy meals. Plan your meals so that you use the most perishable items the first day and the least perishable items by the third day.

Let's say that you are going to market on Monday and Thursday of each week. Dinner on those two nights should consist of items that can be kept the least amount of time without spoiling— chopped meat, poultry, or fresh fish. Use your fresh vegetables on those nights, and rely on frozen or canned vegetables on subsequent nights.

In practice it would work out this way, if you are cooking for two (and while there is a saying, "two can live as cheaply as one," it goes on to say, "if one doesn't eat"). If you are cooking for one, reduce the suggested menu to suit yourself. And if Monday and Thursday do not suit you as the best times to market, use this plan as a guideline and change the marketing days to suit yourself.

Select chopped meat for Monday's dinner, to be used for hamburgers, meat loaf, or meatballs. Select cubes of beef for Tuesday's dinner, for a two-night Beef Bourguignonne (beef stew with wine), to be served on broad noodles Tuesday night and with rice Wednesday night. On Thursday, when you will be marketing for the weekend, choose chicken for Thursday's dinner, deliberately making enough for leftovers to be nibbled during the weekend. Raw chicken should be cooked the first or second day, but cooked chicken that is properly covered and refrigerated may be kept safely for several days. Plan on having a veal or pork dish for Friday night, and cook a potted or roasted beef dish in large enough quantity for Saturday and Sunday.

The following week, have fish Monday and chopped meat on Thursday, with a lamb dish for Tuesday and Wednesday, and a poultry dish for Friday and Saturday. On Sunday, treat yourself to as nice a steak as you can afford.

Using different recipes, this two-week food plan gives you not only variety, but also planned leftovers that merely need to be heated up and served with different food accessories to remain appetizing each time.

Your menu and marketing list would look something like this the first week, with dessert optional:

MENU

Monday: Meat loaf
              Baked potatoes
              Lettuce and tomato salad

Tuesday: Beef Bourguignonne (beef with carrots and mush-
                    rooms)
              Noodles
              Pickled cucumbers

Wednesday: Leftover Beef Bourguignonne, stretched with peas
              Rice
              Canned peach halves with cottage cheese

Thursday: Roasted chicken
              Baked sweet potatoes
              Green beans

Friday: Veal Marsala
              Boiled potatoes with dill (make extra potatoes for
                    potato salad for the weekend)
              Broccoli (fresh or frozen)

Saturday: Roast beef
              Potato salad
              Spinach (frozen)

Sunday:	Sliced roast beef (from Saturday's roast)
	Macaroni and cheese casserole
	Refrigerator roundup salad

MARKETING LIST

	MONDAY	THURSDAY
Meat:	Chopped beef	Chicken
	Cubed beef	Veal for scallopine
		Beef roast
Produce:	Lettuce	Sweet potatoes
	Tomatoes	Green beans (or frozen)
	Potatoes	Broccoli (or frozen)
	Cucumber	Spinach (or frozen)
	Carrots	Fresh fruit
	Mushrooms	
	Fresh fruit	
Container:	Canned tomatoes	Mayonnaise
	Canned peas	Macaroni
	Canned peaches	Cake mix
	Salad dressing	
	Vinegar	
	Broad noodles	
	Rice	
	Cookies	
Dairy:	Milk	Milk
	Eggs	American cheese
	Cottage cheese	Butter or margarine
Bread:	1 Loaf	1 Loaf

The mayonnaise, vinegar, salad dressing, noodles, rice, and macaroni will be used for additional servings in the following weeks, so plan around them to use them up. Every so often stir up a cake mix according to the package directions and pop it into the oven. You will have a fresh inexpensive dessert for several days. Otherwise, serve yourself cheese wedges with fresh fruit, and check off a few more good points for yourself toward your "daily dozen."

Add citrus fruit or juice, cereal, and meat substitutes to this shopping list, and you will be close to achieving a balanced menu. Fill in with a nutritious lunch at your job or on campus, and if you get back to your kitchen for lunch, add sliced cheese, peanut butter, sliced meats, or whatever you prefer to your Monday and Thursday marketing lists.

Get in the habit of writing down your weekly menu, writing your marketing list from it, and adding the extras you think you will need. It's the surest way to economize at the planning stage as you alternate an inexpensive meal or two with an occasional splurge.

Remember, too, that it is better to shop at one food store where you know the layout of the aisles and the quality of the merchandise than to run all over town trying to save a few cents on special items. If your market has a special sale on meat that you haven't considered in your menu for the week, have enough flexibility in your plan to make a substitution. Your menu and marketing list are meant to be good guides rather than strict, confining lists . . . so feel free to make a few changes that will save you money as you shop.

A final word of caution. Supermarkets are built on the premise that consumers will toss many extras into the carts as they market, and the most tempting packages are piled up for just that purpose. Ignore them if you can. Just as daily marketing can wreck your food budget by putting you in contact too often with a magnetic array of goodies, so can your twice-weekly sojourn into the marketplace, if you let it. At least, limit yourself by actual dollar amount to what you will permit as extra purchases that week. The quickest way to stop a food budget leak is to start with a good plan and stick to it!

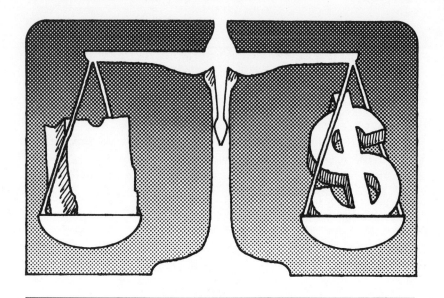

4 · Marketing Strategy

Marketing can turn out to be a lucrative adventure for you. There's a lot of money to be saved if you know what is good quality and what constitutes a poor buy. These are not determined by price alone, but rather by understanding the grading systems that are used and learning how to recognize the best fruit and vegetables available. It makes sense to assume that if you select produce with care, you will be able to keep it fresh and usable for a longer period of time.

There is an art to selecting meat, poultry, and fish too—to get the most edible value for your money. Sometimes a high price will give you more meat and less waste than a bargain cut that is mostly fat and bone. Then again, other cuts of meat, if cooked properly, can put savings in your pocket with every bite.

Here is the kind of information that will make you a marketing "pro" who knows how to select and store food in the most advantageous ways.

ABOUT BUTTER: Butter that is graded by the U.S. Department of Agriculture, and marked with a U.S.D.A. emblem, is your most reliable way of determining quality.

Grade AA is made from high quality fresh sweet cream, has a fine aroma and a delicate sweet taste. Best for table use.

Grade A is also made from cream and must have a pleasing and desirable flavor, although not quite up to the high standards of Grade AA. Good for table use and cooking.

Grade B is generally made from sour cream and is acceptable, although it lacks the fresh flavor of the two finer grades. Avoid for table use but good for cooking.

ABOUT MARGARINE: This spread, which is so like butter in appearance, taste, and function, is manufactured from vegetable or other oils. It is used for reasons of taste preference, economy, or avoidance of animal fats. Sometimes people mistakenly think that margarine has less calories than butter, but actually they have the same calorie count unless it is a "diet margarine" which has less than 80 percent fat and can contain less calories. This must be called "imitation margarine" in the United States.

It's important to read the label of margarine carefully to know exactly what you are buying. Ingredients are listed on the label in order of decreasing amounts. Most often it is made of one or more vegetable oils, but sometimes it also contains animal fat. The liquid is usually pasteurized skim milk, but some are made with water and some with soybean protein fluid. Margarine usually contains from 1½ to 3 percent salt, unless it is clearly stated to be without salt. It always contains an addition of Vitamin A and sometimes has Vitamin D.

Margarine is available in several different forms:

Conventional margarine is commonly sold in one-pound packages of four quarter-pound sticks. It is composed of partially hardened oils and fats and is firm in consistency, suitable for table spread, cooking, or baking.

Soft margarine contains more liquid oil which makes it more spreadable and spoonable. It is usually available in dishlike tubs and packaged in one-pound cartons.

Whipped margarine has been fluffed up in volume with an inert and harmless gas. Since it is expanded by 50 percent it is packed six sticks to a pound, and each helping will contain less fat and calories than the same-size helping of unwhipped margarine. It may be used for general cooking, but do take into consideration that it does not have the same amount of fat per portion as the same-size portion of butter or unwhipped margarine.

Diet margarine contains about half the amount of fat of other margarines. It is called "imitation margarine" simply because it does not meet the U.S. standard for margarine. Because of this reduced fat content it cannot be used for baking without recipe changes, but substitutes nicely as a spread or as a flavoring agent for vegetables.

ABOUT EGGS: Eggs are also graded by U.S.D.A. standards that signify the quality of the eggs but have nothing to do with their size. The size of an egg refers to the minimum weight per dozen, so you may see eggs of all sizes in each grade category.

Grade AA eggs cover a small area when broken on to a flat dish or skillet. Notice that the white is thick and stands high, and that the yolk is firm and stands high.

Grade A eggs cover a moderate area. The white is reasonably thick and stands fairly high, and the yolk is firm and high.

Grade B eggs have none of the above high standards, but are good for general cooking and baking where appearance is not important.

Eggs are weighed by the dozen to determine their size category. A good rule of thumb when buying eggs is to see whether there is less than a 7-cent price spread per dozen eggs between one size and the next smaller size in the same grade. If so, you will get more for your money by buying the larger size:

Jumbo eggs weigh 30 ounces minimum per dozen
Extra Large are   27 ounces minimum per dozen
Large eggs weigh 24 ounces minimum per dozen
Medium eggs are   21 ounces minimum per dozen
Small eggs weigh 18 ounces minimum per dozen
Peewee eggs are   15 ounces minimum per dozen.

Uncovered eggs lose moisture through their porous shells, so store them in the carton or another covered container in the refrigerator. Avoid using egg baskets and door trays that are provided in some refrigerators, unless you intend to use the eggs quickly.

ABOUT POULTRY: If the different designations of chickens confuse you, try to remember that they generally reflect the age und size of the bird. Younger birds are called "broilers" or "fryers" and they are best cooked as their label suggests, but if they are meaty enough, you can roast or pot these young birds. Heavy fowl is more desirable to use for stews and soups, as it is meatier and has a more definite flavor.

Raw poultry may be kept in the refrigerator for one or two days if all plastic wrappings have been removed and the poultry is wrapped in loose waxed paper.

Never leave stuffing in poultry if you are storing it in the refrigerator to use again. The cold of the refrigerator may not penetrate to the center of the bird, and you are courting bacteria growth by refrigerating the stuffing in the bird. Remove it and store in a separate, covered container to be safe.

ABOUT FISH: To tell if a whole fish is really fresh, look at the eyes. If they are bright, clear, and bulging, the fish is fresh. Press the skin if you can; if the pressure leaves no mark of indentation, the fish is fresh. Look at the gills; they should be bright red. Sniff a bit; there should be only a fresh sea odor.

Refrigerate fish immediately and use it within a day for best results.

ABOUT MEAT: Low price should not always be the determining factor when choosing a cut of meat. There is less actual meat in cuts that have a large quantity of bone and fat. A good rule-of-thumb guide when choosing how much to buy to figure adequate portion of meat for one person is:

⅓ pound of boneless meat
½ pound of meat with small amount of bone
1 pound of meat with large amount of bone.

The most expensive cuts of beef are also the tenderest. They come from the loin, rib, and sirloin sections of the animal. Other cuts are less tender and require longer cooking and braising, unless treated with tenderizer or marinated.

Quality beef is generally bright red in color with firm, finely grained fresh and well marbled streaks of white fat. Beef is graded *U.S. Prime, U.S. Choice,* and *U.S. Good* for most home use. U.S. Prime is the finest meat available and the most expensive. U.S. Choice, the grade that is most available in supermarkets, has less fat and is more tender than the lower quality of U.S. Good.

Fresh meat should be loosely wrapped and can be stored in the refrigerator for several days. Ground meat should be used within a day or two. Cured and smoked meats should be wrapped and stored in the refrigerator, and used within a week. Frozen meat should be wrapped airtight and placed in the freezer immediately after purchase. All frozen meat should be stored at 0°F. or lower. It should not be refrozen after defrosting. Frozen meat should not be allowed to defrost unless it is to be cooked promptly. You may keep sausage and ground meat in the freezer from 1 to 3 months; fresh pork, 3 to 6 months; lamb and veal, 6 to 9 months; and beef, 6 to 12 months.

Study the following charts for retail cuts of meat, to be able to recognize the cuts you may see in your butcher's display case. Notice that basic cooking directions are given under each retail cut to guide you to the best method of cooking that cut of meat.

How to Select and Prepare Meat

RETAIL CUTS OF BEEF—WHERE THEY COME FROM AND HOW TO COOK THEM

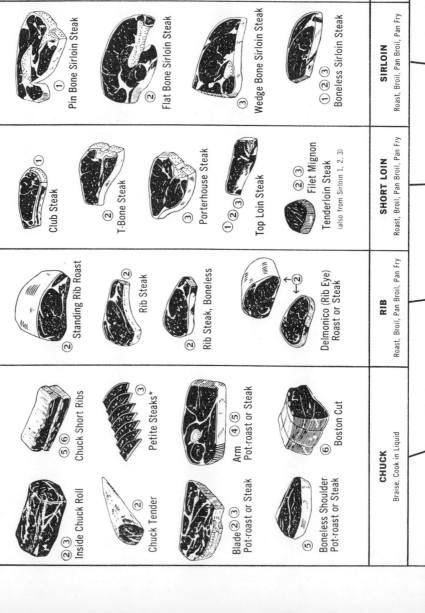

CHUCK	RIB	SHORT LOIN	SIRLOIN	ROUND
Braise, Cook in Liquid	Roast, Broil, Pan Broil, Pan Fry	Roast, Broil, Pan Broil, Pan Fry	Roast, Broil, Pan Broil, Pan Fry	Braise, Cook in Liquid

CHUCK
- ⑤⑥ Chuck Short Ribs
- ②③ Inside Chuck Roll
- ② Chuck Tender
- ③ Petite Steaks*
- Blade ②③ Pot-roast or Steak
- Arm ④⑤ Pot-roast or Steak
- ⑤ Boneless Shoulder Pot-roast or Steak
- ⑥ Boston Cut

RIB
- ② Standing Rib Roast
- ② Rib Steak
- ② Rib Steak, Boneless
- ② Delmonico (Rib Eye) Roast or Steak

SHORT LOIN
- ① Club Steak
- ② T-Bone Steak
- ③ Porterhouse Steak
- ①②③ Top Loin Steak
- ②③ Filet Mignon Tenderloin Steak (also from Sirloin 1, 2, 3)

SIRLOIN
- ① Pin Bone Sirloin Steak
- ② Flat Bone Sirloin Steak
- ③ Wedge Bone Sirloin Steak
- ①②③ Boneless Sirloin Steak

ROUND
- ① Standing Rump*
- ① Rolled Rump*
- Heel of Round
- ③ Round Steak
- ③ Top Round Steak*
- ③ Outside (Bottom) Round Steak or Pot-roast
- ④ Heel of Round
- ③ Eye of Round

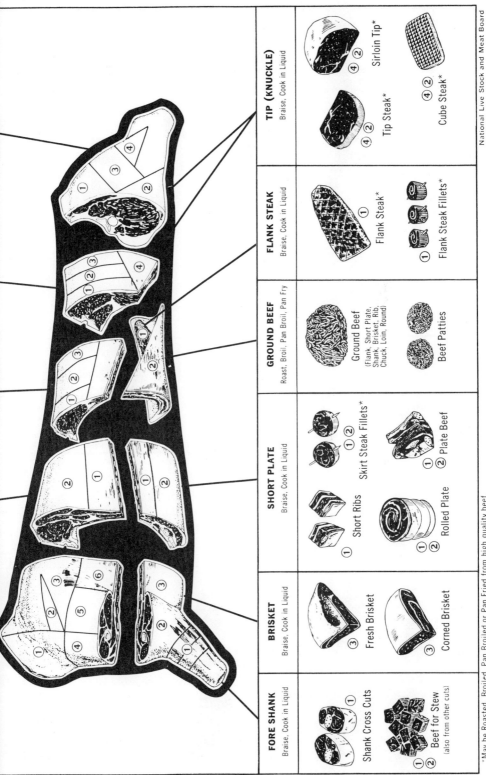

FORE SHANK	BRISKET	SHORT PLATE	GROUND BEEF	FLANK STEAK	TIP (KNUCKLE)
Braise, Cook in Liquid	Braise, Cook in Liquid	Braise, Cook in Liquid	Roast, Broil, Pan Broil, Pan Fry	Braise, Cook in Liquid	Braise, Cook in Liquid

FORE SHANK
① Shank Cross Cuts
① ② Beef for Stew (also from other cuts)

BRISKET
③ Fresh Brisket
③ Corned Brisket

SHORT PLATE
① Short Ribs
① ② Skirt Steak Fillets*
① ② Plate Beef
① ② Rolled Plate

GROUND BEEF
Ground Beef
(Flank, Short Plate, Shank, Brisket, Rib, Chuck, Loin, Round)
Beef Patties

FLANK STEAK
① Flank Steak*
① Flank Steak Fillets*

TIP (KNUCKLE)
④ ② Tip Steak*
④ Sirloin Tip*
④ ② Cube Steak*

*May be Roasted, Broiled, Pan Broiled or Pan Fried from high quality beef.

National Live Stock and Meat Board

RETAIL CUTS OF VEAL—WHERE THEY COME FROM AND HOW TO COOK THEM

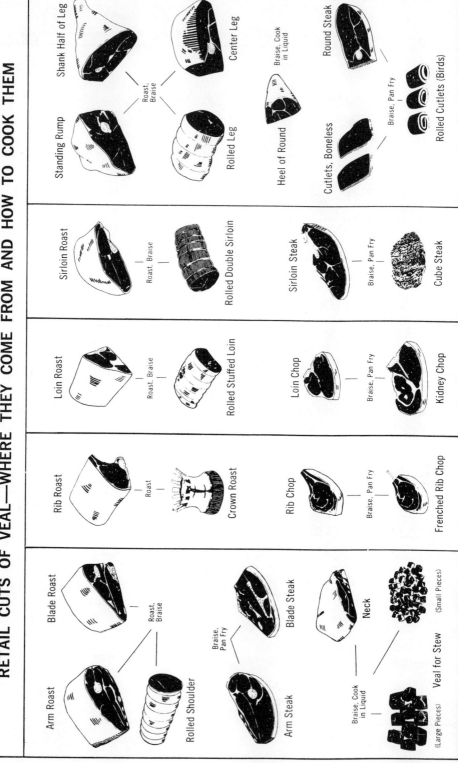

Patties

Roast (bake),
Braise, Pan Fry

Ground Veal

Rolled Cube Steaks (Birds)

Braise

Choplets

Braise, Pan Fry

City Chicken

Mock Chicken Legs

Stuffed Breast

Roast,
Braise

Breast

Stuffed Chops

Braise, Pan Fry

Brisket Pieces

Riblets

Braise, Cook in Liquid

Fore Shank

Braise, Cook in Liquid

Brisket Rolls

Braise

National Live Stock and Meat Board

RETAIL CUTS OF LAMB—WHERE THEY COME FROM AND HOW TO COOK THEM

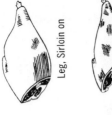 Leg, Sirloin on

 Leg, Sirloin off

 American Leg

 Center Leg

Shank Half of Leg

Leg Chop (Steak)

Rolled Leg

Combination Leg

Sirloin Half of Leg

LEG	Roast, Broil, Pan Broil, Pan Fry

Sirloin Roast

Rolled Double Sirloin

Sirloin Chop

SIRLOIN	Roast, Broil, Pan Broil, Pan Fry

Loin Roast

Rolled Double Loin

English Chop

Loin Chops

LOIN	Roast, Broil, Pan Broil, Pan Fry

 Rib Roast

Crown Roast

Rib Chops

Frenched Rib Chops

RACK	Roast, Broil, Pan Broil, Pan Fry

Arm Chop

Blade Chop

Saratoga Chops

 Square Shoulder

Rolled Shoulder

Cushion Shoulder

 Cubes for Kabobs

 Neck Slices

NECK	Braise, Cook in Liquid

SHOULDER	Roast, Broil, Pan Broil, Pan Fry

FORE SHANK
Braise, Cook in Liquid

Fore Shank

Riblets

BREAST
Roast, Braise, Broil, Pan Broil, Pan Fry, Cook in Liquid

Breast

Rolled Breast

Stuffed Breast

Ribs (for Barbecue, etc.)

Brisket Pieces

Stuffed Chops

HIND SHANK
Braise, Cook in Liquid

Hind Shank

Cube Steak

GROUND OR CUBED LAMB
Roast, Broil, Pan Broil, Pan Fry, Cook in Liquid

(Large Pieces) Lamb for Stew (Small Pieces)

Ground Lamb

Lamburgers

National Live Stock and Meat Board

RETAIL CUTS OF PORK—WHERE THEY COME FROM AND HOW TO COOK THEM

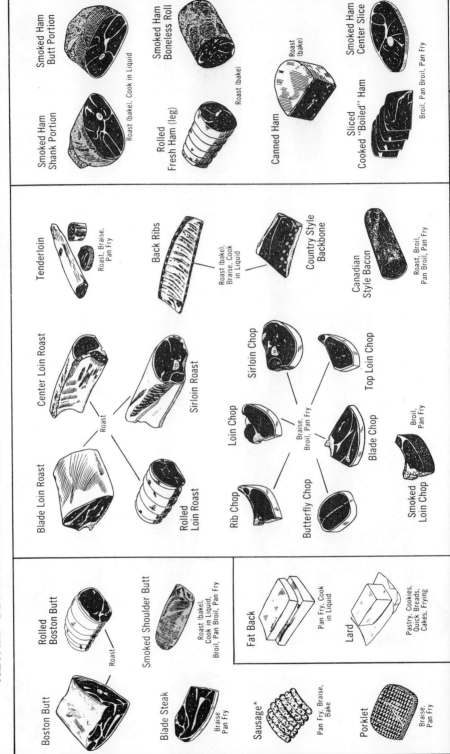

Smoked Ham Shank Portion   **Smoked Ham Butt Portion**

Roast (bake), Cook in Liquid

Rolled Fresh Ham (leg)   **Smoked Ham Boneless Roll**

Roast (bake)

Canned Ham

Roast (bake)

Sliced Cooked "Boiled" Ham   **Smoked Ham Center Slice**

Broil, Pan Broil, Pan Fry

Tenderloin

Roast, Braise, Pan Fry

Back Ribs

Roast (bake), Braise, Cook in Liquid

Country Style Backbone

Canadian Style Bacon

Roast, Broil, Pan Broil, Pan Fry

Blade Loin Roast   **Center Loin Roast**   **Sirloin Roast**   **Rolled Loin Roast**

Roast

Rib Chop   **Loin Chop**   **Butterfly Chop**   **Sirloin Chop**   **Top Loin Chop**   **Blade Chop**

Braise, Broil, Pan Fry

Smoked Loin Chop

Broil, Pan Fry

Boston Butt   **Rolled Boston Butt**

Roast

Smoked Shoulder Butt

Roast (bake), Cook in Liquid, Broil, Pan Broil, Pan Fry

Blade Steak

Braise, Pan Fry

Sausage*

Pan Fry, Braise, Bake

Porklet

Braise, Pan Fry

Fat Back

Pan Fry, Cook in Liquid

Lard

Pastry, Cookies, Quick Breads, Cakes, Frying

Spareribs — Roast (bake), Braise, Cook in Liquid

Salt Pork — Broil, Pan Broil, Pan Fry, Cook in Liquid, Bake

Slab Bacon — Broil, Pan Broil, Pan Fry, Bake

Sliced Bacon

Smoked Picnic — Roast (bake), Cook in Liquid

Canned Picnic — Roast (bake)

Fresh Picnic — Roast

Rolled Fresh Picnic — Roast

Arm Roast — Roast

Arm Steak — Braise, Pan Fry

Fresh Hock — Braise

Smoked Hock — Cook in Liquid

Canned Luncheon Meat* — Roast (bake), Broil, Pan Broil

Jowl Bacon — Cook in Liquid, Broil, Pan Broil, Pan Fry

Pig's Feet — Cook in Liquid, Braise

*These items may come from several areas of the pork side.

National Live Stock and Meat Board

ABOUT CANNED FOOD: Avoid the purchase of any can that has bulging ends, deep dents, or rust marks. If you open a can that has an off-odor or signs of mold, don't even taste the contents—just throw it out!

Food in cans kept in a cool place will remain fresh and usable for six months to a year and sometimes longer. Learn to read labels with care to find out exactly what you are buying. Ingredients are listed in order of amount in the can, so if you are buying a canned beef stew, for instance, look to see that the beef is listed first. Otherwise, you may have a full plate of vegetables for dinner with a dab of meat here and there, when you would prefer it the other way about.

ABOUT FROZEN FOOD: Avoid the purchase of any packages that seem soft to the touch. Buy only in a market that has a good turnover, and reach down in open cases for packages that are near the bottom of the freezer case. Do not buy packages that are piled above the safety line (look for it) in an open case, as they have been handled too much and are not in a position to remain safely frozen.

Use a thermometer to test your refrigerator's freezer compartment—if it does not reach 0°F., it is not safe for longer than a few days' storage.

Be sure everything that is placed in the freezer is wrapped airtight. Use heavy-duty plastic bags, aluminum foil, and plastic freezer containers to achieve airtight wrapping.

ABOUT VEGETABLES: Buy only the amount that you will use within a short period of time, as vegetables are highly perishable. Sort the vegetables before storing, and discard any that are bruised, soft, or decayed. Here is a list that will help you get the most food return for your money, with additional advice on how to store each kind of vegetable:

Asparagus:	Stalks should be mostly green with compact tips. Remove tough white parts of stalks. Store in refrigerator crisper in a plastic bag. Use within 1 or 2 days.
Beans, Lima:	Select well-filled pods that are clean, fresh, and of good color. Old and tough beans will

have shriveled, spotted, or flabby pods. Shelled lima beans should be plump and of good green or green-white color. Refrigerate and use within 1 or 2 days.

Beans, Snap: Select pods with small seeds, as overmature pods may be tough. Avoid dry-looking or wilted pods. Refrigerate and use within 1 or 2 days.

Beets: Select smooth and firm beets. Soft or shriveled beets may be tough. Store beets, covered, in the refrigerator, and use within 1 or 2 weeks.

Broccoli: Select stalks that are clean with compact green clusters. Avoid those with yellow flower clusters. The stalks should be dark green, tender, and firm. Dirty spots may indicate insects. Store in refrigerator in a plastic bag and use within 1 or 2 days.

Brussels Sprouts: Select firm sprouts of good green color. Avoid those that have worm-eaten or wilted leaves, or a dirty appearance. Store in the refrigerator in a plastic bag and use within 1 or 2 days.

Cabbage: Select crisp, firm heads that feel heavy for their size. Avoid those that are discolored, soft, or have wormholes. Store in plastic bag in the refrigerator and use within 1 or 2 weeks.

Carrots: Select those of good color that are smooth and firm. Avoid wilted or shriveled carrots, large-size ones that may have a pithy core, and those that are cracked. Remove tips and tops and store in a plastic bag in the refrigerator for 1 to 2 weeks.

Cauliflower: Select a white, clean, firm, and compact head with fresh green leaves. Avoid spotted or bruised heads. Store, covered, in the refrigerator and use within 3 to 5 days.

Celery:	Select crisp, clean celery with branches that will snap easily. Avoid soft, pithy, or stringy stalks. Wrap in plastic bag and store in crisper of refrigerator. Use within 1 or 2 weeks.
Corn:	Select ears with plump kernels and fresh green husks. Avoid dry or yellowed husks. Cook as soon after purchase as possible.
Cucumbers:	Select firm, green, well-shaped cucumbers. Avoid those that are withered or overmature, and those that have decay spots. Store in refrigerator crisper and use within 3 to 5 days.
Eggplant:	Select firm, dark-purple, heavy eggplant. Avoid those that are soft or scarred. Decay appears as brown spots on the surface. Store in a cool place (60°F.) or store in refrigerator in a plastic bag.
Lettuce:	Select crisp, clean heads that are firm and heavy for their size. Avoid those that have rust spots and those with an excess of outer leaves. Wash and dry before storing; wrap in paper toweling and store in crisper of refrigerator. Use within 1 or 2 days.
Mushrooms:	Select clean, white, firm mushrooms with light-colored gills on the underside. Avoid dark and discolored mushrooms. Store in a plastic bag in the refrigerator and use within 1 or 2 days.
Onions:	Select clean, hard onions with dry skins; avoid those with developing seed-stem and those that feel moist at the neck, which is an indication of decay inside. Store in a cool place at 60°F. and they will keep for a month or so.
Parsley:	Select bright-green, crisp-appearing leaves; avoid yellowing wilted-looking leaves. Wash thoroughly, shake dry, and place in a tightly

covered jar in the refrigerator. Use within 1 or 2 weeks.

Peas: Select light-green, firm, and well-filled pods; avoid flat, wilted, or yellowing pods. Store in pods in refrigerator until wanted. Use within 1 or 2 days.

Peppers: Select firm, fresh-colored peppers; avoid shriveled, spotted, or dull-appearing ones. Wash and dry. Store in crisper in the refrigerator and use within 3 to 5 days.

Potatoes: Select firm, smooth, well-shaped potatoes; avoid sprouting, wilted, leathery, or discolored ones. Keep at room temperature and in a dark place for 3 to 4 weeks. When they are exposed to light, the exposed portion turns green and may taste bitter.

Radishes: Select smooth, firm, crisp radishes of good color; avoid wilted, decayed, and pithy ones. Remove tops and store in a plastic bag in the crisper of the refrigerator. Use within 1 to 2 weeks.

Spinach: Select leaves that are clean, crisp, and fresh-green in color; avoid wilted, bruised, and yellowed leaves. Decay appears as a slimy spot. Wash and dry. Wrap in paper toweling and store in the crisper of the refrigerator. Use within 1 or 2 days.

Tomatoes: Select well-formed plump and uniformly red ones; avoid those that have bruise marks or are soft or discolored. Store uncovered in the refrigerator crisper. Keep unripened tomatoes at room temperature, away from direct sunlight until ripe, and then refrigerate. Use within 3 to 5 days.

Zucchini: Select crisp, dark-green zucchini; avoid soft spots, mold growth, and wilted appearance. Wash, dry, and wrap in plastic. Store in refrigerator. Use within 3 to 5 days.

Apples: Select firm, well-colored fruit; avoid those that lack good color, those that are bruised or decayed, and those that have a shriveled appearance. Overripe apples yield to slight pressure on the skin, and will have soft, mealy flesh. Store unripe or hard apples at cool room temperature (69° to 70°F.) until ready to eat. Store mellow apples, uncovered, in the refrigerator, and use within a week.

Apricots: Select plump, uniform-colored golden-orange, juicy-looking fruit; avoid those that are bruised or decayed, dull-looking, pale yellow or greenish-yellow in appearance. Store ripe fruit, uncovered, in the refrigerator. Use within 3 to 5 days.

Avocados: Select slightly soft fruit that yields to gentle pressure on the skin; avoid those with dark sunken spots, or those with cracked or broken surfaces. When unripe, allow to ripen at room temperature, not in direct sunlight. Store ripe fruit, uncovered, in the refrigerator, and use within 3 to 5 days.

Bananas: Select yellow, firm fruit; avoid those with decay marks. Bananas with green tips have not developed their fullest flavor; those with brown flecks have. Store at room temperature.

Blueberries: Select plump, firm, uniform-size berries; avoid those that are soft, bruised, or discolored. Keep in the refrigerator for use within 1 to 2 days. Wash just before using.

Cherries: Select well-colored fruit with bright, glossy, plump-looking surfaces; avoid those with shriveled appearance, dried stems, and soft, leaking flesh with brown discolorations. Wash just before using. Use within 1 or 2 days.

Cranberries:	Select plump, firm berries, with good red color; avoid soft, spongy, or leaky berries as they may be of poor flavor. Store in refrigerator for 1 or 2 days, and wash just before using.
Grapefruit:	Select firm, well-shaped fruit that seems heavy for its size; avoid those with soft discolored areas on the peel near the stem end, and peel that breaks easily under finger pressure, as they are signs of internal decay. They are picked "tree-ripe," so store in the refrigerator and use within 5 to 7 days.
Grapes:	Select well-colored, plump grapes that are firmly attached to the stem, which itself should be green and pliable. Avoid soft or wrinkled grapes with whitened areas around the stem end, and leaking grapes, which are a sign of decay. Refrigerate and use within 1 or 2 days.
Lemons:	Select those that have a rich yellow color, a smooth-textured skin, and feel firm and heavy for their size. Avoid lemons that are off-color, dull in appearance, and those with hard or shriveling skin or soft spots. Refrigerate and use within 1 week.
Limes:	Select limes with glossy skin; they should feel firm and heavy for their size. Avoid those with dull, dry skin, and those with soft spots, mold, and skin breaks. Store in the refrigerator and use within 1 week.
Melons:	*Cantaloupes (Muskmelons).* Select those with well-defined netting marks and a background color that is yellowish. The melon should yield slightly to thumb pressure on the blossom end; avoid overripeness that is indicated by a soft rind, and avoid those that are bruised or have mold near the stem scar. Full maturity is indicated by a pleasant melon odor noticeable when fruit is held to the nose.

Casaba. Select those with a golden-yellow rind and a slight softening at the blossom end; avoid those with dark, sunken, or water-soaked spots, as this indicates internal decay.
Honey Ball and Honeydew. Select melons of yellowish-white to creamy rind color, with slight softening at the blossom end, and a pleasant aroma. Avoid those with dead-white or greenish-white color, smooth rather than velvety feel, and bruised or punctured appearance.
Persian. Follow selection procedure used with cantaloupes.
Watermelons. Look for smooth surface with a slight dullness of color and a cream-colored underbelly. If cut, select those with good red color, firm flesh, free from white streaks, and with seeds that are dark brown or black. Avoid pale-colored flesh, whitish seeds (which indicate immaturity) and mealy or watery flesh.

All melons should be kept at room temperature until ripened and should be refrigerated until used. Use within 1 or 2 days.

Nectarines: Select plump, rich-colored fruit with a slight softening along the seam; avoid hard, dull-colored fruit, shriveled and soft fruit, or over-ripe fruit with signs of decay. Store at room temperature until ripe, then store in the refrigerator until ready to use. Use within 3 to 5 days.

Oranges: Select firm fruit with fresh and bright-looking skin. Avoid those that are lightweight for their size, have dull, dry skin, or pitted skin and discolored appearance. Refrigerate and use within 5 to 7 days.

Pears: Select those that have begun to soften but have a firm appearance. Avoid wilted fruit with dull-looking skin and weakness of skin near the stem. Ripen at room temperature and refrigerate until wanted. Use within 3 to 5 days.

Pineapples:	Select fruit that is heavy for its size, those of good color for the variety, and those whose leaves can easily be pulled out. Avoid those with dried appearance, bruises or discolorations, an unpleasant odor, or traces of mold. Pineapples will ripen at room temperature, and should then be refrigerated until wanted. Use within 1 to 2 days.
Plums and Prunes:	Select fruit of a good color for the variety, and those that feel slightly soft to the touch. Avoid fruit with discolorations or breaks in the skin, and those that are leaking or decaying. Store in refrigerator until wanted. Use within 3 to 5 days.
Strawberries:	Select those with full, red color and firm flesh, with stem intact and a dry, clean appearance. Avoid berries that are soft, bruised, or discolored. Keep whole in the refrigerator until ready to use. Wash just before using. Use within 1 to 2 days.
Tangerines:	Select those of deep orange color and good luster. Avoid those that are off-color or greenish, and those with any signs of decay. Refrigerate until wanted, and use within 5 to 7 days.

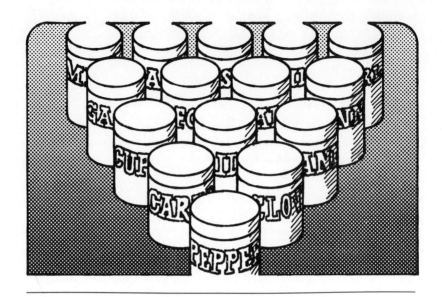

5 · Subtlety in Seasoning

Cooking becomes really creative when you master the use of a few herbs and spices that complement the ingredients of your meal. The recipes in this book make liberal use of a variety of these seasonings to help you learn by practical experience how a dash of this and a dash of that will enhance your meals.

Buy herbs and spices in small quantities and keep them in a cool, dry place. Be sure that the containers are tightly closed, especially the ones with shaker holes that you may carelessly leave open when you are in a hurry. Try to keep your spices together—if they are lined up on a rack, place them in alphabetical order so you can find them quickly as you cook. If you keep them in an upper cabinet near the range, place them on a circular rack with some system so you can revolve the rack and pluck out the spice you need with ease.

In the beginning, there is a great temptation to use too much of one, or too many different kinds of seasonings in one dish. The great puzzle with herbs and spices is to find out which ones go well together and which are not compatible. Following recipes carefully is one way to learn the proper amounts to use and the tasty combinations that may be made. If you are "winging it" and cooking as you go, just remember to use small pinches of seasonings—they do go a long way.

Here is a list of popular seasonings that describes their taste and how best to use them to improve the flavor of your cooking.

Allspice:

A sharply flavored berry that is dried and ground into a powder that tastes like a combination of cinnamon and cloves. Another product called All-spice—notice the hyphen—is a blend of many spices, including cinnamon, cloves, and nutmeg. Both can be used to enhance the flavor of fruit, such as in pies; and in some meat dishes.

Basil, Sweet:

Although a member of the mint family, this leaf has a sweetish flavor. It enhances tomato dishes, soups and salads, and Italian-style sauces.

Bay Leaf:

A dried leaf of the laurel family, it has a strong aromatic flavor and is especially good with potted meats and hearty meat soups.

Caraway:

The small aromatic seeds of a parsley-type plant, it is used to flavor bread, cheese, cabbage dishes, and some meat dishes.

Cardamon:

A seed that is sold both ground and whole, it is a member of the ginger family and has a sweet, pungent taste. It is also spelled cardamum and cardamom. It is frequently used in Indian and Scandanavian cooking, in curries, and in pastries.

Cayenne Pepper:

This is also called red pepper or chili pepper. It is ground into a powder from the fruit of the capsicum plant. The powder is very hot with a biting taste and may be used sparingly in some meat dishes, cheese dishes, and spicy sauces.

Chervil:

Has an anise flavor and is a member of the parsley family. It may be used in soups, egg dishes, and in some vegetable dishes.

Chili Powder: A powdered blend of spices that has been created to enhance the flavor of Mexican cooking. The basic ingredients are chili pepper, oregano, cumin, and garlic, sometimes with cloves and allspice added. Use in sauces, stews, and meats for south-of-the-border flavor.

Chives: Hollow green tips of an onion-family plant that have a subtle onion taste. Use in salads, with sour cream for baked potatoes, in delicate sauces, and in some cheese dishes.

Cinnamon: Has an aromatic, sweet-pungent taste and is available in stick form or ground into a fine powder. Made from the bark of several trees, including the cassia in the United States, it is used to complement fruit in pastries and compotes, and in meat dishes in many Middle Eastern countries.

Cloves: An aromatic, pungent-tasting, dried bud that is available both whole and ground. It has a warm spicy flavor that can enhance pickled dishes, ham, tongue, desserts, mulled wines, and teas.

Coriander: A member of the parsley family; its leaves are used in salads, soups, and stews. The seeds of the plant are also used and have a lemon-sage flavor that is used in curries, pastries, and some meat dishes.

Cumin: A nutty-flavored seed that is related to the parsley family. It is available whole or ground and is an ingredient of chili powder and curry powder. It adds a pungent flavor to Middle Eastern recipes for soups, cabbage dishes, and fish and meat dishes.

Curry Powder: A blend of many spices ground together, it has a hot, spicy flavor. It usually contains cayenne, coriander, cumin, turmeric, and sometimes allspice, cinnamon, ginger, and pepper. It is used in Indian-style cooking, for soups, sauces, stews, and seafood dishes.

Dill: A member of the parsley family, this herb has a recognizable odor and flavor. The stem and leaves of the plant are available as "dillweed" and the seeds as "dillseed." They are used in pickling, soups, seafood and chicken dishes, and are especially tasty in cream sauces.

Garlic: Has a strong and distinct odor and flavor, and is available as a bulb with many cloves, or in powder or salt form. Rub a cut clove on a salad bowl for subtle flavor, and use it to season meats, seafood, chicken, and sauces. Very nice mixed with butter and spread on Italian or French bread before heating.

Ginger: Has a sweet and spicy flavor and is obtained from the root of a tropical plant. It is available ground or in slivers, and is used to flavor cooked fruits, pastry, sauces, some Far Eastern-style meat dishes, and some vegetable dishes.

Mace: A powder ground from the membrane of the fruit of the nutmeg tree. It has a flavor similar to nutmeg—warm and spicy but a little more pungent. It is lighter in color than nutmeg and is frequently used in light-colored dishes. Can be used in baking, sauces, pumpkin dishes, and in some meat, vegetable, and fish dishes.

Marjoram: A member of the mint family, this leaf has a sweet, tangy taste and is available whole or ground. It is used in some vegetables, soups, lamb dishes, and in stuffings.

Mint: An aromatic herb of the mint family, most popularly known as spearmint. This leaf is used in jellies, sauces, candies, meat dishes, and some desserts.

Mustard: Prepared from the mustard seed in powdered or paste form. It has a hot, sharp flavor and is used in cheese, meat, and fish dishes, and as a condiment for sandwiches.

Nutmeg: A seed that has a sweet, spicy flavor, and is available in whole or ground form. It is used in baking, puddings, sauces, some vegetables, and some meat dishes.

Oregano: A member of the mint family, this leaf has a strong but pleasantly bitter taste. It is used frequently in Italian and Mexican cooking and is especially good in tomato sauces, eggs, cheese, and meat dishes.

Paprika: A fine, red powder with a slightly sweet taste, made from the fruit of a variety of red pepper, it is used both to decorate and flavor food. It is especially popular in Hungarian cuisine, and may be used as a garnish, on roasts, on poultry, and in soups.

Parsley: An herb with distinctly aromatic-tasting leaves. Available fresh, or dried and chopped. Used as a garnish for its lacy leaves, and as a seasoning for fish, meat, soups, and sauces.

Pepper: A dried, pungent berry that is available in whole form, known as "peppercorns," or ground. Black pepper is obtained from the entire berry and has a more intense taste, while white pepper is ground after the outer covering of the seed is removed. White pepper is used where a more subtle flavor is desired, and where the food is light in color. It is used to flavor soups, sauces, meat of all kinds, and vegetables.

Rosemary: The dried or fresh leaf of a mint-family plant, this has a sweet flavor and is especially good in lamb dishes, vegetables, sauces, and soups.

Saffron: A spice that is made from the dried golden stigmas of a variety of crocus, it is used sparingly for its slightly bitter taste and as a yellow coloring agent for food. Very popular in Spanish, French, and Italian dishes that contain rice. Also used in some sauces and soups.

Sage:	The leaves of this pungent, slightly bitter-tasting member of the mint family are usually dried and ground. Use to season stuffings, some soups, sauces, and meat dishes. Adds distinction to vinegar marinades.
Savory:	Available in two varieties. Summer Savory is more subtle in taste than Winter Savory, which has a thyme-like flavor. Savory is a member of the mint family and is used in vegetables, sauces, and egg cookery.
Tarragon:	Aromatic leaves that have a slightly licoricelike flavor. Used to enhance sauces, chicken, eggs, and some meat dishes.
Thyme:	A member of the mint family that has a warm, aromatic flavor. It is frequently used in chowders, poultry stuffings, with tomatoes, and in some cheese and fruit dishes.
Turmeric:	A member of the ginger family, this is an important ingredient of curry powder. It is used in curries, fish dishes, sauces, and for pickling.

Since each spice and herb has an affinity for certain vegetables and fruits, here is a helping-hand checklist for you to use to help you determine compatibility. It's like having your own computer-dating list for each seasoning!

Allspice:	Beets, cabbage, carrots, eggplant, spinach, tomatoes, yellow squash, apples, cherries, cranberries, figs, peaches, and rhubarb.
Basil, Sweet:	Asparagus, beans, beets, broccoli, brussels sprouts, cabbage, carrots, cauliflower, celery, onions, peas, potatoes, spinach, summer squash, tomatoes, white turnips, yellow turnips, and zucchini.
Bay Leaf:	Beets, cabbage, carrots, potatoes, and tomatoes.
Caraway:	Cabbage, potatoes, and white turnips.
Cardamon:	Carrots, onions, peas, sweet potatoes, apples,

	cherries, cranberries, figs, grapefruit, oranges, peaches, pears, pineapple, and rhubarb.
Cayenne Pepper:	Beans, tomatoes, and corn.
Chervil:	Carrots, peas, and spinach.
Chili Powder:	Carrots, eggplant, onions, potatoes, and white turnips.
Chives:	Beans, cauliflower, mushrooms, peas, potatoes, and tomatoes.
Cinnamon:	Sweet potatoes, yellow squash, apples, apricots, blueberries, cherries, cranberries, figs, grapefruit, peaches, pears, pineapple, plums, prunes, and rhubarb.
Cloves:	Beets, cabbage, carrots, yellow squash, apples, apricots, blueberries, cherries, cranberries, lemon, lime, peaches, pears, plums, prunes, and rhubarb.
Coriander:	Artichokes and tomatoes.
Cumin:	Cabbage, corn, and cucumbers.
Curry Powder:	Beans, broccoli, brussels sprouts, cabbage, corn, onions, potatoes, and summer squash.
Dill:	Beans, beets, brussels sprouts, cabbage, carrots, eggplant, potatoes, spinach, tomatoes, and white turnips.
Garlic:	Onions, mushrooms, potatoes, and tomatoes.
Ginger:	Carrots, onions, peas, sweet potatoes, apples, cherries, cranberries, figs, grapefruit, peaches, pears, pineapple, and rhubarb.
Mace:	Carrots, potatoes, spinach, sweet potatoes, apples, peaches, and pineapple.
Marjoram:	Asparagus, beets, brussels sprouts, carrots, celery, onions, peas, spinach, summer squash, tomatoes, and zucchini.
Mint:	Beans, beets, carrots, peas, potatoes, spinach, melon, oranges, and pineapple.

Mustard:	Cabbage, celery, cucumber pickles, peas, spinach.
Nutmeg:	Asparagus, beans, beets, broccoli, brussels sprouts, cabbage, carrots, cauliflower, onions, peas, spinach, summer squash, sweet potatoes, yellow squash, apples, blueberries, cherries, cranberries, grapefruit, lemon, lime, pineapple, and rhubarb.
Oregano:	Beans, broccoli, eggplant, mushrooms, onions, peas, spinach, tomatoes, and zucchini.
Paprika:	Cauliflower, corn, onions, and potatoes.
Parsley:	Asparagus, beets, eggplant, mushrooms, potatoes, tomatoes, and zucchini.
Pepper:	Beans, cabbage, celery, eggplant, onions, peas, potatoes, spinach, tomatoes, and zucchini.
Rosemary:	Carrots, cauliflower, eggplant, mushrooms, onions, peas, potatoes, spinach, summer squash, white turnips, and yellow turnips.
Saffron:	Rice.
Sage:	Brussels sprouts, eggplant, onions, potatoes, summer squash, and tomatoes.
Savory:	Asparagus, beans, brussels sprouts, eggplant, and yellow turnips.
Tarragon:	Asparagus, beets, cabbage, mushrooms, and tomatoes.
Thyme:	Asparagus, beans, beets, carrots, eggplant, mushrooms, onions, potatoes, spinach, tomatoes, white turnips, yellow turnips, and zucchini.
Turmeric:	Cauliflower, peas, and tomatoes.

BASIC HERBS AND SPICES: It is likely that you will never have occasion to use many of these seasonings in your cooking, but it helps to know what they are when you do need them. For everyday cooking the following herbs and spices are the ones you will use over and over again. Buy them in small quantities to keep them in fresh supply and add others as they are called for in recipes you want to try.

Basil
Bay Leaf
Chili Powder
Cinnamon
Cloves
Curry Powder
Dill
Garlic (salt or powder will do)
Ginger
Mustard
Nutmeg
Oregano (if you like Italian-style cooking)
Paprika
Parsley, dried
Pepper

6 · The Vital Vocabulary

Don't let a word stop your cooking prowess. Look it up in this list of kitchen terminology and you will be able to understand any recipe in any cookbook. It's a necessary addition to your language if you are going to do your own cooking.

Bake:　　　To bake food means to put it in the oven and cook it with indirect dry heat. 350°F. is considered medium heat, 250°F. is low, and 450°F. is high. Your oven should have an indicator on it with degrees shown for accurate baking temperatures.

Barbecue:　　Usually means to cook over an open fire, but also can refer to the spicy seasoning used on roasted or broiled meats.

Baste:　　Refers to the process of spooning gravy, fat, or wine over baking or roasting food that is in the oven. Basting prevents food from drying out if it is uncovered.

Beat: Stir food together until smooth; to do it right, think of a fast-moving tune. A waltz just won't do!

Blanch: The process you use to remove the skin of fruit, vegetables, or nuts. Immerse the food in boiling water for a minute—then quickly into icy water to stop the cooking action and shed the skin. With this technique it slips off at the flick of a sharp knife.

Blend: Stir two or more ingredients together until they become one. Do it with a cooking spoon, or better still, with an electric blender. No need to beat air in—just beat identity out!

Boil: If it's liquid and it bubbles while it's cooking—it's boiling. Gentle bubbles are called a low-boil, and vigorous bubbles are called a rapid-boil. If you are directed to bring something to a boil, cook it until it bubbles.

Braise: This refers to a method of cooking in which you brown the meat on all sides in hot fat, and then add a small amount of liquid, cover the pot, and simmer over low heat for long, slow cooking. Method is usually used for less tender cuts of meat.

Bread: When used as a verb it means to dip food in crumbs until it is completely covered. An easy way to do this is to put the crumbs in a plastic bag and then shake the food inside the bag, one piece at a time, until coated.

Brew: This refers to a method of extracting flavor from food by letting it stand in hot water until the water is flavored.

Broil: Put the food on an open pan under direct heat, gauging the distance from the heat by the thickness of the food. The thinner the food, the closer to the source of heat you can put it. Watch out for fat flare-ups, but if you suddenly see your steak in flames—reach for the salt and throw a handful in: salt is one of the few things that will put a fat fire out fast.

Candy: When used as a verb it means to glaze with a sugary syrup. It's a toothsome way to coat fruits and vegetables.

Caramelize: A method of cooking sugar over low heat until it melts and turns light brown. Remember to stir constantly and remove from heat before it burns.

Chop: To cut food in fine pieces either with a food chopper in a wooden bowl or in an electric blender. A slower way is to use a knife—and keep your fingers away from the blade!

Cream: Don't add cream unless it's called for—this is a verb that means to mix fat until it is fluffy. It can be done with the back of a spoon, but an electric mixer is better.

Cube: Cut the ingredient into small squares.

Cut: Use a knife and divide food as directed. Also used to describe a method of making pastry, where the fat is "cut" into the flour until small particles of the mixture result.

Devil: You just know it's going to be hot! It refers to the addition of condiments to food to give it a spicy taste.

Dice: Similar to cube, except it's on a smaller scale.

Dredge: Sounds like hard work, but it isn't. Just refers to coating food with flour until the entire surface is covered. Use a plastic bag, as in *Bread.*

Dust: Sprinkle food lightly with sugar or flour, just enough to cover with a fine film. The food will definitely not be as well covered as in *Bread* or *Dredge.*

Fillet: If it's a verb—remove the bones. If it's a noun—they're already out.

Flake: Using a fork, break a solid piece of food into flat pieces. *Flake off* means the same thing, so don't leave!

Flambé: Set the food ablaze with spirits high in alcohol. Follow directions carefully or there will be a fireman in your future.

Fold:	This method of combining foods is used when it is important not to destroy air bubbles, as with a soufflé or sponge-cake batter. Mix the food from the bottom of the bowl to the top by bringing a cooking spoon down the back of the bowl, through the ingredients at the bottom of the bowl in a direction toward you, and then up the front of the bowl, across the top toward the back of the bowl, then down the back of the bowl again. Repeat in slow motion until the ingredients are combined. Don't stir, mix, or beat, as the mixture will flatten as the air escapes.
Fricasee:	When you stew meat in gravy for a long time, in a covered pot over low heat—you're doing it!
Fry:	Refers to cooking in melted fat. "Deep-fry" means that there is a large enough quantity of fat to cover the ingredients you want to cook. Be sure that the ingredients do not have water on them or you will have spatter burns to remind you of your indiscretion.
Glaze:	A cooking technique that is used when you want to cover food with a mixture that will create a shiny surface.
Grate:	In order to reduce a food to tiny particles, you must rub it against a rough cutting surface with tiny wires or holes—the process is called "grating," the heap of particles are "grated," and the gadget you are using is a "grater."
Grill:	When you cook by broiling on a rack, or over an open fire, you are grilling.
Grind:	A way of reducing food to small particles with a food chopper or blender.
Julienne:	This refers to food that is cut in slender strips—if it's in cubes or balls, it is not julienne!
Knead:	The action required to fold and stretch dough until it becomes smooth and elastic. It may be done with your hands, or if you are lucky, with the dough hook on an electric mixer. An electric beater won't do it.

Lard:	As a noun it means fat. As a verb it means to cover meat or fish with strips of fat—and sometimes it means inserting bits of fat into meat with a larding needle.
Marinate:	Think of "soak" and you'll understand. This refers to a technique used to tenderize and flavor meat, and the mixture it is soaking in is called the "marinade."
Mince:	It means chop it very fine.
Mix:	As a verb, combine foods together. As a noun referring to "mix" or "mixture," it is already combined.
Mold:	This is the way to get food to retain a particular shape—pour it into a shaped container until chilled, frozen, or set according to directions, and then remove it from the container.
Pan broil:	Cook in an uncovered skillet, pouring off fat as it accumulates so you are not frying.
Pan fry:	Cook in an uncovered skillet in a small amount of fat so food will be crisp.
Parboil:	This refers to a method of cooking food part way in boiling water to prepare for cooking further by another method.
Pare:	When you cut the skin off fruits and vegetables, you are doing it.
Peel:	Removal of the skin of a fruit that can be stripped by hand.
Poach:	A method of cooking that refers to simmering over low heat in a hot liquid.
Puree:	When food is reduced to a smooth sauce in a blender or through a food mill, the sauce is called a "puree."
Reduce:	To boil a liquid down to a smaller quantity and stronger intensity.
Render:	The heating of fat until it melts and can be poured off separated from all connective tissue.

Roast:	Can be done over an open fire, but in the home it means to cook in the oven.
Roux:	A thickening mixture that is formed by cooking flour and butter together and then adding it to the food to be thickened.
Sauté:	Another word for fry, but this time in a smaller amount of fat, over lower heat, and for a shorter amount of time.
Scald:	Heat liquid to a point just below boiling—you've done it just before the bubbles break!
Score:	Cut lines across the surface of food just before roasting, or around the edges of a steak just before broiling.
Sear:	Seal in the juices of meat by browning fast either over high heat or in a very hot oven. When you have "seared" in the juices, the heat is reduced for further cooking.
Simmer:	Cook in liquid over low heat that is just below the boiling point. Used for delicate results.
Skewer:	As a verb, it is the piercing of food onto a long pin before cooking. As a noun, it is the long pin itself.
Skim:	Take a spoon and remove fatty substances that are floating in your cooking liquid. When it refers to milk, the fatty substances have already been removed.
Sliver:	Cut food in slender pieces of small size.
Steam:	A method of cooking food suspended over boiling water.
Stew:	If it's a verb, cook food in liquid over low heat for a long time. If it's a noun, it refers to ingredients already cooked that way.
Stir:	Combine ingredients together with a slow circular motion until blended.
Whip:	Beat ingredients rapidly, to add air and inflate the volume of the mixture. If you are whipping cream, be sure to stop the moment the shiny mixture

breaks into a thick dull one—one moment too much and you will have the beginnings of butter.

WEIGHTS AND MEASURES

AMOUNT		EQUIVALENT
⅓ of ½ teaspoon	•	A pinch
½ of ¼ teaspoon	•	⅛ teaspoon
3 teaspoons	•	1 tablespoon
2 tablespoons	•	⅛ cup
4 tablespoons	•	¼ cup
5 tablespoons plus 1 teaspoon	•	⅓ cup
8 tablespoons	•	½ cup
10 tablespoons plus 2 teaspoons	•	⅔ cup
12 tablespoons	•	¾ cup
16 tablespoons	•	1 cup
1 cup	•	8 fluid ounces
2 cups	•	1 pint
2 pints	•	1 quart
4 cups	•	1 quart
2 quarts	•	½ gallon
4 quarts	•	1 gallon
16 ounces, dry measure	•	1 pound
32 ounces, fluid measure	•	1 quart
¼ pound of butter	•	½ cup
1 pound of butter	•	2 cups
½ pound Cheddar cheese	•	2 cups grated
3 ounces of cream cheese	•	6 tablespoons
1 pound flour	•	4 cups sifted
1 pound cake flour	•	4¾ cups sifted
1 medium lemon	•	3 tablespoons juice
1 medium lemon rind	•	1 tablespoon grated rind
1 medium orange	•	⅓ cup juice
1 medium orange	•	2 tablespoons grated rind
1 pound unshelled walnuts	•	1⅔ cups chopped nuts
1 pound granulated sugar	•	2½ cups
1 pound brown sugar	•	2⅓ cups
1 pound confectioners' sugar	•	3½ cups
1 cup raw rice	•	3 cups cooked

7 · Exciting Eggs

Eggs can be kinder to your budget than any other form of protein. And that doesn't mean that your palate will suffer while you are saving, for eggs can be the basis of delicious cooking. This chapter has many recipes to prove it to you, and to inspire you to invent some omelets of your own. Those dabs of leftovers that you are tempted to throw away can be blended into a fluffy omelet instead —giving you a delicious, low-cost dish. It's no crime to let the garbage pail go hungry!

There are a few pointers that will help you to cook eggs better:

1. Always cook eggs over low heat so they don't get tough.

2. Eggs separate better when they are cold, but the whites beat higher when they are at room temperature. A few grains of salt expand the volume too.

3. To boil eggs, choose a saucepan that won't darken (aluminum always does) and that is deep enough so that water will

cover the eggs completely but still not splash over during cooking.

4. To boil eggs, bring the water to a boil first, and then reduce the heat to a low simmer. Place eggs in the water with a slotted spoon. Cook soft-cooked eggs for 2 to 4 minutes, depending on how solid you prefer them; and cook hard-cooked eggs for 12 to 15 minutes. Rinse immediately under cold water and the shells will slip off with no trouble at all.

5. To poach eggs, use a skillet full of boiling water. Add a teaspoon of vinegar to the water and reduce the heat. Stir a circle in the water and break an egg into the circle; push spreading white back over the yolk with a spoon until it solidifies. Cook for about 4 minutes. Remove egg with a slotted spoon and serve on toast or English muffin.

6. To fry eggs, heat butter in a skillet until melted. Break each egg carefully into the skillet and cook until done the way you like it. Turn over with a spatula if you prefer your egg "once over lightly," or just spoon a bit of white over the yolk and cover for a moment until a thin film forms. Remove eggs with a spatula.

7. To scramble eggs, heat butter in a skillet and pour in beaten eggs. Let egg mixture solidify around the edges and then gently push the cooked egg toward the center to permit the uncooked mixture to flow around the edges and set. Avoid any vigorous stirring as the mixture will crumble into tiny particles. Remove from heat when the mixture is still moist, or it will be overcooked by the time you serve it.

8. Cover leftover raw egg whites and refrigerate safely for several days. Place leftover raw egg yolks in a small container, cover with water, and refrigerate covered for several days; or poach them in water and sieve them as a flavorful garnish over cooked vegetables.

COTTAGE SCRAMBLE

To serve 2:	To serve 4:	
AMOUNT	AMOUNT	INGREDIENTS
4	8	Eggs
1/2 teaspoon	1 teaspoon	Salt
Dash	1/8 teaspoon	Pepper
1 tablespoon	2 tablespoons	Butter
1/2 cup	1 cup	Cottage cheese
1 tablespoon	2 tablespoons	Chopped parsley

Mix eggs, salt, and pepper with a fork. Heat butter in a large skillet. Pour in egg mixture. Reduce heat enough to cook eggs quickly, lifting mixture from the bottom and sides as it thickens. As the cooked mixture is lifted, the thin uncooked part should flow to the bottom. Avoid constant stirring. When eggs are almost thickened throughout, stir cottage cheese into egg mixture. The cheese will melt and coat the scrambled eggs. Remove from heat as soon as cheese is melted, garnish with parsley, and serve at once.

Here's an emergency dish that almost jumps from the refrigerator into the frying pan! A catsup base gives a taste surprise to the protein life-saver on top.

SCRAMBLED EGG RAFTS

To serve 2:	To serve 4:	
AMOUNT	AMOUNT	INGREDIENTS
3	6	Eggs
2 tablespoons	1/4 cup	Milk or light cream
1/4 teaspoon	1/2 teaspoon	Salt
Dash	1/8 teaspoon	Pepper
2 teaspoons	1 tablespoon	Butter
2 slices	4 slices	Toast
2 tablespoons	4 tablespoons	Catsup
1/4 cup	1/2 cup	Shredded Cheddar cheese

Mix eggs, milk, salt, and pepper with a fork. Heat butter in a skillet just hot enough to sizzle a drop of water. Pour in egg mixture. As mixture begins to set at bottom and sides, gently lift cooked portions with a spatula so that the thin, uncooked part can flow to the bottom. Avoid constant stirring. Cook until eggs are thickened throughout, but still moist.

Spread hot toast with catsup. Place toast on baking sheet and spoon scrambled eggs on each piece. Sprinkle with cheese and place under broiler for a moment until cheese melts. Serve at once.

HASHED OMELET

To serve 2:	To serve 4:	
AMOUNT (FILLING)	AMOUNT (FILLING)	INGREDIENTS
1/4 cup	1/2 cup	Chopped onion
1 tablespoon	2 tablespoons	Butter
1/2 can	1 can (15 1/2-ounce)	Corned beef hash
2 tablespoons	1/4 cup	Pickle relish
AMOUNT (OMELETS)	AMOUNT (OMELETS)	
4	8	Eggs
1/4 cup	1/2 cup	Water
1/2 teaspoon	1 teaspoon	Salt
1/4 teaspoon	1/2 teaspoon	Pepper
2 teaspoons	4 teaspoons	Butter

Cook onion in butter until tender, but not browned. Stir in corned beef hash and pickle relish. Stir ingredients to mix; heat through. When mixture is piping hot, remove from heat and set aside while preparing omelets.

For each omelet: Mix 2 eggs, 2 tablespoons of water, ¼ teaspoon salt, ⅛ teaspoon of pepper. Heat 1 teaspoon of butter in an omelet pan (8-inch size) just hot enough to sizzle a drop of water. Pour in egg mixture. Mixture should set at edges at once. With a spatula or a fork, carefully draw cooked portions toward center, so that the uncooked portions flow to the bottom. Slide pan rapidly back and forth over the heat to keep mixture in motion and sliding freely. Keep mixture as level as possible. When eggs are set and surface is still moist, increase heat to brown bottom quickly.

To serve, place ½ cup of hash mixture on each omelet. Fold omelet over hash and slide onto plate. Make one filled omelet for each serving.

STRAWBERRY-CHEESE OMELET

To serve 2:	To serve 4:	
AMOUNT (FILLING)	AMOUNT (FILLING)	INGREDIENTS
1 package (3-ounce)	2 packages	Cream cheese
1/2 package	1 package (1 pound)	Frozen strawberries
AMOUNT (OMELETS)	AMOUNT (OMELETS)	
4	8	Eggs
1/4 cup	1/2 cup	Water
1/2 teaspoon	1 teaspoon	Salt
2 teaspoons	4 teaspoons	Butter

Drain strawberries, reserving liquid. Blend together cream cheese with ¼ cup strawberry syrup (2 tablespoons of syrup for the recipe that serves 2) until smooth. Set aside. Omelets are made individually.

For each omelet: Mix 2 eggs, 2 tablespoons of water, and ¼ teaspoon salt. Heat 1 teaspoon of butter in an omelet pan (8-inch size) just hot enough to sizzle a drop of water. Pour in egg mixture. Mixture should immediately set at edges. With a spatula or a fork, carefully draw cooked portions toward center, so that the uncooked portions flow to the bottom. Slide pan rapidly back and forth over the heat to keep mixture in motion and sliding freely. Keep mixture as level as possible. When eggs are set and surface is still moist, increase heat to brown bottom quickly. Remove pan from heat and spread cream cheese mixture over half of omelet; fold and slip out onto serving plate. Top with strawberries and serve at once.

Keep a can of cherry pie filling on your shelf for an emergency occasion when you want to serve something sweet and filling. Everything else will come from staples. Start the coffee first so the serving will be smooth.

RED CHERRY OMELET

To serve 2:	To serve 4:	
AMOUNT (FILLING)	AMOUNT (FILLING)	INGREDIENTS
1/4 cup	1/2 cup	Canned red tart cherry pie filling (22-ounce can)

AMOUNT (OMELETS)	AMOUNT (OMELETS)	
4	8	Eggs
1/4 cup	1/2 cup	Water
1/2 teaspoon	1 teaspoon	Salt
2 teaspoons	4 teaspoons	Butter
Several dashes	Several dashes	Confectioners' sugar

Heat pie filling through, and set aside. Omelets are made individually.

For each omelet: Mix 2 eggs with 2 tablespoons of water and ¼ teaspoon salt. Heat butter in an 8-inch omelet pan just hot enough to sizzle a drop of water. Pour in egg mixture. Mixture should immediately set at edges. With a spatula or fork, carefully draw cooked portions at edges toward center, so that uncooked portions flow to the bottom. Slide pan rapidly back and forth over heat to keep mixture in motion and sliding freely. When eggs are set and surface is still moist, increase heat to brown bottom quickly. To serve, spoon hot cherry pie filling on half of omelet. Fold omelet and sprinkle with confectioners' sugar. Serve at once.

DANISH EGG SALAD SANDWICH

To serve 2:	To serve 4:	
AMOUNT	AMOUNT	INGREDIENTS
3	6	Hard-cooked eggs
1/4 cup	1/2 cup	Finely chopped celery
1 1/2 teaspoons	1 tablespoon	Finely chopped onions
2 tablespoons	1/4 cup	Mayonnaise
1 1/2 teaspoons	1 tablespoon	Vinegar
1/8 teaspoon	1/4 teaspoon	Tabasco sauce
1/2 teaspoon	1 teaspoon	Salt
2 slices	4 slices	White or rye bread
1 teaspoon	2 teaspoons	Softened butter
2	4	Lettuce leaves
Dash	Dash	Paprika

Slice hard-cooked eggs, reserving one whole center slice for each sandwich as garnish. Chop remaining eggs and put in a bowl. Add celery and onion and toss lightly. Stir vinegar, Tabasco, and salt into mayonnaise until well blended. Pour dressing over egg mixture and stir until moistened throughout. Spread each slice of bread with butter. Cover bread with lettuce. Scoop egg salad on top of lettuce, and top each scoop with a reserved egg slice. Dash paprika over all.

BAKED EGGS 'N' CANADIAN BACON

To serve 2 or 3:	To serve 4 to 6:	
AMOUNT	AMOUNT	INGREDIENTS
2 tablespoons	1/4 cup	Butter
2 tablespoons	1/4 cup	Diced green pepper
2 tablespoons	1/4 cup	Pimiento strips (optional)
2 tablespoons	1/4 cup	Flour
3/4 cup	1 1/2 cups	Water
6 tablespoons	3/4 cup	Instant nonfat dry milk
1 cube	2 cubes	Chicken bouillon
1/2 teaspoon	1 teaspoon	Worcestershire sauce
1/4 teaspoon	1/2 teaspoon	Salt

To serve 2 or 3:	To serve 4 to 6:	
AMOUNT	AMOUNT	INGREDIENTS
Dash	Dash or two	Pepper
3 slices	6 slices	Canadian bacon
3	6	Hard-cooked eggs, halved
1/4 cup	1/2 cup	Shredded Swiss cheese

Melt butter in a saucepan; sauté green pepper until tender. Stir in pimiento and flour. Remove from heat; gradually stir in water; then nonfat dry milk, bouillon cubes, Worcestershire sauce, salt, and pepper. Cook over medium heat, stirring constantly, until thickened. Cook 2 additional minutes. Trim fat from Canadian bacon slices; place in a shallow baking dish in a single layer; top each slice with 2 egg halves; pour sauce over all. Bake in a preheated 350°F. oven for 15 minutes. Top with shredded cheese; return to oven for about 3 minutes more. Serve at once.

BAKED DEVILED EGGS

To serve 2 or 3:	To serve 4 to 6:	
AMOUNT	AMOUNT	INGREDIENTS
1 can (8-ounce)	2 cans	Tomato sauce
1 tablespoon	2 tablespoons	Brown sugar
1 1/2 teaspoons	1 tablespoon	Chopped onions
1/8 teaspoon	1/4 teaspoon	Ground thyme
3	6	Hard-cooked eggs
1 1/2 teaspoons	1 tablespoon	Mayonnaise
1/2 teaspoon	1 teaspoon	Wine vinegar
1/4 teaspoon	1/2 teaspoon	Prepared mustard
1/4 teaspoon	1/2 teaspoon	Salt
Dash	1/8 teaspoon	Pepper

Pour tomato sauce into a flat baking dish, reserving 1 tablespoon per can used. Add brown sugar, onion, and thyme to sauce and mix well. Cut eggs in half lengthwise. Remove yolks and mix with the reserved sauce, mayonnaise, vinegar, mustard, salt, and pepper. Fill egg whites with this mixture and place in sauce. Bake at 350°F. for 20 to 25 minutes, or until tops of eggs are lightly browned and sauce bubbles. Serve on hot buttered rice or toast.

HOT DOG EGGWICH

| To serve 2: | To serve 4: | |
AMOUNT	AMOUNT	INGREDIENTS
1	2	Frankfurters, sliced into thin rounds
1/2 tablespoon	1 tablespoon	Butter
2	4	Eggs
2 tablespoons	1/4 cup	Milk
1/4 teaspoon	1/2 teaspoon	Salt
Dash	1/8 teaspoon	Pepper
2	4	Buttered frankfurter rolls

Lightly brown frankfurters in butter. Mix eggs, milk, salt, and pepper; mixing thoroughly for a uniform yellow, or mixing slightly if streaks of white and yellow are preferred. Pour egg mixture over frankfurter slices. As mixture begins to set at bottom and sides, gently lift cooked portions with a spatula so that the thin, uncooked part can flow to the bottom. Avoid constant stirring. Cook until eggs are thick but still moist, about 3 to 5 minutes. Spoon onto buns.

At a loss for something to serve for brunch? Here's an egg dish that is blended with a velvety cream sauce. Serve it over toast triangles, chow mein noodles, or rice.

EGGS AND MUSHROOMS IN CHEESE SAUCE

| To serve 2 or 3: | To serve 4 to 6: | |
AMOUNT	AMOUNT	INGREDIENTS
1/8 pound (about 3/4 cup)	1/4 pound	Mushrooms, sliced
1 1/2 teaspoons	1 tablespoon	lemon juice
2 tablespoons	4 tablespoons	Butter
1/4 cup	1/2 cup	Chopped celery
1/4 cup	1/2 cup	Chopped green pepper
2 tablespoons	1/4 cup	Chopped onions
1 tablespoon	2 tablespoons	Flour
1/4 teaspoon	1/2 teaspoon	Salt

To serve 2 or 3:	To serve 4 to 6:	
AMOUNT	AMOUNT	INGREDIENTS
Dash	Dash or two	Pepper
1/2 cup	1 cup	Milk
1/2 cup	1 cup	Shredded Cheddar cheese
1/8 teaspoon	1/4 teaspoon	Worcestershire sauce
2	4	Hard-cooked eggs

Toss mushrooms with lemon juice. In a large skillet melt butter; add mushrooms, celery, green pepper, and onion; sauté until almost tender. Stir in flour, salt, and pepper. Remove from heat; gradually stir in milk. Cook over medium heat, stirring constantly, until thickened. Cook 2 additional minutes. Remove from heat; add cheese and Worcestershire sauce; stir until cheese is melted. Set aside one egg yolk; chop remaining eggs and add to sauce. Heat mixture to serving temperature, but do not boil. Sieve remaining egg yolk as a garnish over the top.

CREAMED EGGS AND CHICKEN

To serve 2:	To serve 4:	
AMOUNT	AMOUNT	INGREDIENTS
2 slices	4 slices	Toasted white bread
1/2 can	1 can (4 3/4-ounce)	Chicken spread
2	4	Hard-cooked eggs, quartered
1/2 can	1 can (10 1/2-ounce)	Condensed cream of mushroom soup
Dash	Dash	Paprika

Spread toast with chicken spread; top each slice with 4 egg quarters. Place in a warm oven. Heat condensed soup to boiling; pour over eggs. Sprinkle with paprika. Serve at once.

ASPARAGUS-EGG BAKE

To serve 2 or 3: AMOUNT	To serve 4 to 6: AMOUNT	INGREDIENTS
2/3 cup	1 1/3 cups	Bread crumbs
1 tablespoon	2 tablespoons	Melted butter
2 tablespoons	4 tablespoons	Butter
2 tablespoons	4 tablespoons	Flour
1/2 teaspoon	1 teaspoon	Salt
1/2 cup	1 cup	Milk
1/2 cup	1 cup	Asparagus liquid
1/2 cup	1 cup	Grated American cheese
1 can (14 1/2-ounce)	2 cans	Green asparagus, drained
2	4	Hard-cooked eggs, sliced
1 jar (4 1/2-ounce)	2 jars	Sliced mushrooms, drained
1 tablespoon	1 tablespoon	Dried parsley flakes

Toss bread crumbs with melted butter. Set aside. Then make a
sauce by melting the additional butter. Stir flour and salt into the
melted butter and gradually add milk and asparagus liquid. Cook
over medium heat, stirring constantly, until mixture thickens, and
then add grated cheese and stir until it is melted and smooth. In a
flat buttered casserole dish, layer half of the asparagus, sliced eggs,
sauce, mushrooms, and bread crumbs in that order. Repeat the
layer and top with chopped parsley. Bake at 350°F. for 30 minutes.

CORN-APPLE BREAD WITH CREAMED EGGS

To serve 8: AMOUNT FOR BREAD	INGREDIENTS
1/4 cup	Butter
1	Medium onion, chopped
1	Green pepper, seeded and chopped
1 package (18-ounce)	Corn muffin mix
2	Eggs, well beaten
2 cups	Canned apple sauce
1 teaspoon	Powdered poultry seasoning

2 cans (10 1/2 ounces each)	Condensed cream of celery soup
1/2 cup	Dairy sour cream
1/4 cup	Chopped, drained pimiento
8	Hard-cooked eggs, sliced
1/4 teaspoon	Salt

Melt butter in a skillet; sauté onion and green pepper until tender. Add this mixture and pan drippings to corn muffin mix. Add eggs, apple sauce, and poultry seasoning. Stir until well blended. Pour mixture into a well-greased 9-inch-square pan; bake in a 400°F. oven for 35 to 40 minutes, or until lightly browned.

While bread is baking, mix celery soup, sour cream, and pimiento in a large saucepan. Cook over low heat, stirring constantly until well blended and hot. Gently stir in eggs and salt. Cut bread in squares and spoon eggs over.

For brunch, lunch, or any other munch-time, here's a dish that has earned its fame. If the Hollandaise Sauce seems too tricky, try a Hollandaise sauce mix available in package form.

EGGS BENEDICT

To serve 2:	To serve 4:	
AMOUNT	AMOUNT	INGREDIENTS
2	4	Poached eggs
2	4	Thin slices ham
1	2	English muffins, split and lightly toasted

HOLLANDAISE SAUCE:

1/4 cup	1/2 cup	Butter
1	2	Egg yolks, beaten
1/8 teaspoon	1/4 teaspoon	Salt
1 tablespoon	2 tablespoons	Lemon juice

Poach eggs according to directions on page 55. Place a slice of ham on each toasted muffin half, tucking the edges under to conform with the round shape. Top each ham slice with a poached egg and cover with several tablespoons of Hollandaise Sauce.

To make Hollandaise Sauce, place about ⅓ of the butter in the top of a double boiler over hot water. Add egg yolk and beat constantly with a wire whisk. As the butter is blended, add more of the butter until it is all thick and smooth. Remove from heat and stir in salt and lemon juice. Mixture may be kept for a short while over hot (but not boiling) water.

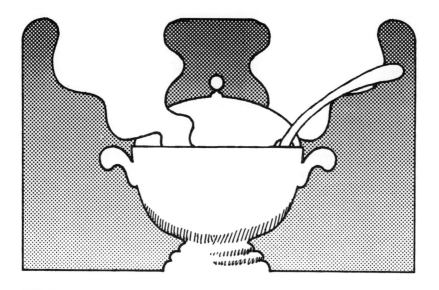

8 · Substantial Soups

Of all the food courses that reveal your culinary compassion, soup seems to do it best! Soup can give comfort and sustenance when needed—without requiring too much pot-watching to achieve. Have soup as a late-night snack, a hearty sandwich accompaniment, as well as a first or second course to dinner.

What makes soup? A couple of bones, with clinging meat for flavor, a few vegetables, a sprinkling of this and that seasoning, and a lot of water are all it takes to get the pot started. You can even start with a can or a package of convenience food soup and, if you wish, add a few quick tricks to make your own delectable invention.

Homemade soup requires a gentle skimming of fatty residues now and then during cooking, with a final removal of the solidified block of fat after you have refrigerated the brew. Tightly covered, soup can last all week, going from refrigerator to stove as the spirit moves you. Add leftover vegetables and bits of cut-up meat and chicken if you wish to change its character. And don't pour the liquid from canned vegetables down the drain—pour it into your soup jar instead. The idea is rather reminiscent of the old soup kettle on the back of the peasant's stove, that kept changing flavor as new additions of scraps of meat and vegetables were added to the always simmering, always welcoming pot.

Keep a supply of bouillon cubes on hand for those recipes that call for a cup of broth—pop a cube in boiling water and, voilà, you have a cup of broth. So nice to live in the convenience generation.

Because soup has a cordiality of its own, it's nice to ladle it from a tureen if you are serving guests. Somehow it makes the event more important and even the soup gains in stature. Drop in a few croutons (do you know that they are available already toasted and even flavored with garlic?) or some popcorn as a garnish, float a thin slice of lemon, or sprinkle some chopped chives for a change of pace. You'll be "right on" every time.

SALMON CHOWDER

To make 1 quart:	*To make 2 quarts:*	
AMOUNT	AMOUNT	INGREDIENTS
1/2 can	1 can (1-pound)	Tomatoes
1/2 cup	1 cup	Peeled, diced potatoes
1/2 cup	1 cup	Peeled, diced carrots
3 tablespoons	1/3 cup	Chopped onions
1 1/2 tablespoons	3 tablespoons	Butter
1 tablespoon	2 tablespoons	Chopped green pepper
1 can (8-ounce)	1 can (1-pound)	Pink salmon, drained
1/2 can	1 can (10 1/2-ounce)	Condensed cream of celery soup
1 1/2 cups	3 cups	Milk

In a saucepan combine tomatoes, potatoes, carrots, onion, butter, and green pepper; cover and simmer for 30 minutes or until vegetables are tender. Meanwhile, remove skin and bones from salmon; break into chunks. In saucepan, gradually add milk to soup; stir in salmon. Heat over low heat, stirring occasionally. When vegetables are tender, slowly add vegetables to salmon-milk mixture (do not boil). Serve hot.

ORANGE-TOMATO SOUP

To serve 2 or 3:	*To serve 4 to 6:*	
AMOUNT	AMOUNT	INGREDIENTS
1 1/2 cups	3 cups	Orange juice
1 can (10 3/4 ounce)	2 cans	Condensed tomato soup
2 tablespoons	4 tablespoons	Dairy sour cream
1 teaspoon	2 teaspoons	Chopped chives

Blend orange juice with tomato soup, stirring until smooth. Heat to serving temperature. Garnish with a dollop of sour cream and chopped chives.

CELERY NOODLE SOUP

To serve 4 to 6:

AMOUNT	INGREDIENTS
1 can (10 1/2-ounce)	Condensed cream of celery soup
1 can (10 1/2-ounce)	Condensed chicken noodle soup
1 1/2 cups	Water
1/2 cup	Milk
1 teaspoon	Dried minced parsley

In a saucepan, empty contents of both cans of soup. Add water, milk, and dried parsley; stir until smooth. Heat, stirring now and then. Serve hot.

HEARTY BEAN SOUP

To serve 4 to 6:

AMOUNT	INGREDIENTS
1 can (11 1/4-ounce)	Condensed split pea with ham soup
1 can (11 1/2-ounce)	Condensed bean with bacon soup
2 soup cans	Water
1/4 cup	Garlic croutons

In a saucepan, empty contents of soup cans; add water and stir until smooth. Heat, stirring occasionally. Ladle into soup bowls and garnish with croutons.

CELERY-CARROT SOUP

To serve 2 or 3:	To serve 4 to 6:	
AMOUNT	AMOUNT	INGREDIENTS
1 can (10 1/2-ounce)	2 cans	Condensed cream of celery soup
1 can (8-ounce)	1 can (1-pound)	Sliced carrots
1/2 soup can	1 soup can	Water
1/8 teaspoon	1/4 teaspoon	Dried dill

Empty can of soup into a saucepan; add carrots with juice. Add water and dill. Heat together, stirring occasionally. Serve at once.

CREAM OF TOMATO-RICE SOUP

To serve 2 or 3:	To serve 4 to 6:	
AMOUNT	AMOUNT	INGREDIENTS
1 can (10 1/2-ounce)	2 cans	Condensed cream of tomato soup
1 can (8-ounce)	1 can (1-pound)	Stewed tomatoes
1/2 soup can	1 soup can	Water
1/4 cup	1/2 cup	Minute rice

Empty tomato soup into a saucepan. Add stewed tomatoes and water. Add rice. Heat to boiling point, then cover and simmer for several minutes, stirring occasionally. Serve at once.

SPINACH SOUP SUPREME

To serve 4 to 6:	
AMOUNT	INGREDIENTS
1 package (10-ounce)	Frozen chopped spinach in cream sauce, cooked
1 can (10 1/2-ounce)	Condensed cream of chicken soup
2 cups	Milk
Dash	Nutmeg

Combine cooked creamed spinach with soup in a saucepan. Add milk and nutmeg. Stir until smooth. Heat and serve. Top with a dollop of sour cream, if desired.

CREAM OF CORN SOUP

To serve 4 to 6:

AMOUNT	INGREDIENTS
1 can (1 pound)	Creamed corn
2 cups	Milk
1 tablespoon	Butter
1/4 teaspoon	Salt
1/8 teaspoon	Pepper

Empty creamed corn into a saucepan; add milk, butter, salt, and pepper. Simmer several minutes, until the butter is melted, stirring occasionally. Serve at once.

POTATO SOUP

To serve 4 to 6:

AMOUNT	INGREDIENTS
4	Large peeled potatoes, diced
1	Onion, diced fine
2 stalks	Celery, diced fine
3 cups	Water
2 cups	Milk
1/2 teaspoon	Salt
1/4 teaspoon	Pepper
1/2 teaspoon	Dried dill
2 tablespoons	Butter
2 tablespoons	Freeze-dried chives

Place potatoes, onion, celery, water, and milk in a saucepan. Add salt, pepper, and dried dill. Simmer for 20 minutes until potatoes are soft; stir in butter until melted. Ladle into bowls and top with generous sprinklings of chives.

CABBAGE-AND-TOMATO SOUP

To serve 4 to 6:

AMOUNT	INGREDIENTS
4	Meaty neck bones, beef
1 can (2-pound)	Tomatoes
4 cups	Water
1/2	Small head of cabbage, shredded
1	Apple, peeled and diced
2 tablespoons	Brown sugar
3 tablespoons	Lemon juice
3/4 teaspoon	Salt
1/4 teaspoon	Ginger

Place bones, tomatoes, water, cabbage, and apple in a saucepan. Add brown sugar, lemon juice, salt, and ginger. Simmer for 2 hours, covered. Skim fat off surface occasionally. Serve with chunks of meat in each bowl.

MEATY PEA SOUP

To serve 4 to 6:

AMOUNT	INGREDIENTS
3 or 4	Meaty neck bones of beef
6 cups	Water
1 cup	Split peas
1 large	Onion, sliced
4	Whole scraped carrots, cut in half
1 teaspoon	Salt
1/4 teaspoon	Pepper
1	Bay leaf

Place neck bones of beef in a deep saucepan; cover with 6 cups of water. Add split peas, sliced onion, and carrots. Add salt, pepper, and bay leaf. Simmer for 2 hours, stirring occasionally, until meat is tender and peas are distintegrated. Remove bay leaf. For informal feasting, serve with pieces of meat in the soup.

CHICKEN SOUP WITH BROAD NOODLES

To serve 6 to 8:

AMOUNT	INGREDIENTS
1 (4-pound)	Chicken
2 quarts	Water
1 large	Onion, peeled
4	Whole carrots, scraped
4	Celery stalks, including tops
2 sprigs	Parsley
2 sprigs	Dill (fresh)
2 teaspoons	Salt
1/4 teaspoon	Pepper
1 teaspoon	Sugar
1/2 pound	Broad noodles

Place cleaned chicken in a deep kettle; add water. Add onion, carrots, celery, parsley, and dill. Season with salt, pepper, and sugar; bring to a boil, then simmer covered until the chicken is tender, about 2 hours. Remove chicken, onion, carrots, celery, and greens. Skim off excess fat. Cook broad noodles according to package directions; drain and place some in each soup bowl. Ladle hot soup over noodles. Add chunks of cooked chicken and carrots to each bowl.

ONION SOUP

To serve 4 to 6:

AMOUNT	INGREDIENTS
3 large	Onions, sliced thin
2 tablespoons	Butter
4	Beef bouillon cubes
4 cups	Boiling water
1/2 teaspoon	Salt
1/8 teaspoon	Pepper
1/4 cup	Parmesan cheese, grated

In a saucepan, sauté onions in butter until translucent. Dissolve bouillon cubes in boiling water and add to onions. Add salt and pepper. Simmer for 20 minutes, covered. Ladle into small deep bowls and top each with a good serving of grated Parmesan cheese.

After you've carved a turkey, don't throw the carcass away! Instead, make this excellent turkey stock that you can refrigerate and use for the interesting recipes that follow.

TURKEY STOCK

To make 4 cups of stock:

AMOUNT	INGREDIENTS
3 pounds	Turkey bones with clinging meat
6 cups	Water
1 stalk	Celery with leaves, cut up
1	Small onion, peeled and quartered
1	Carrot, peeled
1	Bay leaf, crushed
1 teaspoon	Salt
2	Whole cloves
1/4 teaspoon	Ground pepper

Break up turkey carcass and place in a large saucepot with a cover. Add water, celery, onion, carrot, bay leaf, salt, cloves, and pepper. Cover and bring to boil; reduce heat and simmer 3 to 4 hours, turning bones occasionally. Strain. Remove meat from bones and add to stock. If necessary, add sufficient water to make 4 cups. Chill. Remove fat layer from top before using.

TURKEY SOUP ROYALE

To serve 2 or 3:	*To serve 4 to 6:*	
AMOUNT	AMOUNT	INGREDIENTS
2 tablespoons	4 tablespoons	Butter
2 tablespoons	1/4 cup	Flour
1/2 teaspoon	1 teaspoon	Salt
Dash	1/8 teaspoon	Pepper
1 1/2 cups	3 cups	Milk
1/2 cup	1 cup	Turkey stock
1	2	Hard-cooked eggs, finely chopped

To serve 2 or 3:	To serve 4 to 6:	
AMOUNT	AMOUNT	INGREDIENTS
1/2 package	1 package (10-ounce)	Frozen peas and carrots, cooked and drained
1/2 cup	1 cup	Cut-up cooked turkey

In a saucepan, melt butter; stir in flour, salt, and pepper. Remove from heat; gradually stir in milk and turkey stock until smooth. Cook over medium heat, stirring constantly, until thickened. Cook 2 additional minutes. Stir in eggs, vegetables, and turkey; heat to serving temperature. Serve at once.

MULLIGATAWNY SOUP

To serve 2 or 3:	To serve 4 to 6:	
AMOUNT	AMOUNT	INGREDIENTS
1/4 cup	1/2 cup	Butter
1/8 teaspoon	1/4 teaspoon	Curry powder
1/4 cup	1/2 cup	Chopped onion
1/4 cup	1/2 cup	Chopped celery
1/4 cup	1/2 cup	Sliced scraped carrots
1 tablespoon	2 tablespoons	Chopped green pepper
3 tablespoons	6 tablespoons	Flour
1/2 teaspoon	1 teaspoon	Salt
Dash	Dash or two	Nutmeg
Dash	Dash or two	Ground cloves
1 1/2 cups	3 cups	Milk
1/2 cup	1 cup	Turkey stock
1 cup	2 cups	Cut-up cooked turkey
1/2 cup	1 cup	Chopped unpeeled apple

In a saucepan with cover, melt butter. Stir in curry powder, onion, celery, carrots, and green pepper; sauté 5 minutes. Stir in flour, salt, nutmeg, cloves, milk, turkey stock, turkey, and apple. Simmer, covered, for 10 minutes. Serve at once.

CREAM OF VEGETABLE SOUP

To serve 2 or 3:	To serve 4 to 6:	
AMOUNT	AMOUNT	INGREDIENTS
1/2 package	1 package (10-ounce)	Frozen mixed vegetables
2 tablespoons	1/4 cup	Butter
2 tablespoons	1/4 cup	Flour
3/4 teaspoon	1 1/2 teaspoons	Salt
1/4 teaspoon	1/2 teaspoon	Sage
Dash	1/8 teaspoon	Pepper
1 1/4 cups	2 1/2 cups	Milk
1/2 cup	1 cup	Turkey stock
1/2 cup	1 cup	Cut-up cooked turkey

Cook vegetables according to package directions. Meanwhile, in a saucepan melt butter; stir in flour, salt, sage, and pepper. Remove from heat; gradually stir in milk and turkey stock. Cook over medium heat, stirring constantly, until thickened. Cook 2 additional minutes. Stir in vegetables with liquid and turkey. Heat to serving temperature but do not boil.

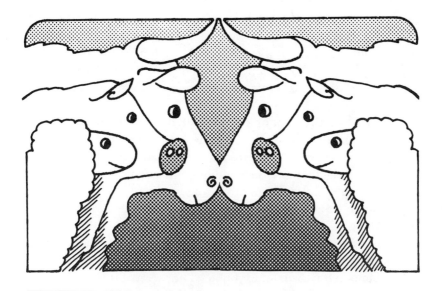

9 · Prudent Meats

No matter how you slice it, meat is usually the most expensive food item on your marketing list. So it's wise to learn as much as you can about the different cuts of meat and what to do with them in the kitchen. Use the meat charts (see pp. 21–29) to become familiar with the various cuts. Many markets use their own terminology to identify special cuts of higher-priced steaks. Don't hesitate to ask exactly what part of the carcass is being sold to you. Often, if you learn how to tenderize and marinate certain less expensive cuts of meat, you will be able to enjoy a good dinner and a good saving at the same time.

Your first judgment should be based on how much actual edible meat and how much bone and fat are contained in the piece of meat you are thinking of buying. Boneless meat may appear to be more expensive, but when you take the amount of waste into consideration you will find that with bony and fatty cuts you are often paying more per pound of edible meat.

Next, cast an appraising eye on the color of the fat surrounding the beef. The whiter it is, the better the grade. Then look at the beef itself and notice whether there is a fine network of fat grained throughout the meat—if there is, it will be a tender cut. If the meat is poorly trimmed, you will be paying meat prices for fat waste, so watch out for those steaks that have large wedges of fat framing the beef.

Veal, being the meat of a young calf, has little fat graining, but the color of the meat usually tells the story. Look for veal that is pinkish-white in color, and avoid the older grayed-out or getting-red colors. What fat there is should be white and firm, and the bone marrow should look young and porous.

When buying lamb, look for pale pink lean meat as it is a sign of a young milk-fed animal. The color darkens with age and becomes known as mutton when the animal reaches 20 months old. The fat should be a waxy white and firm to the touch. Unless you prefer lamb that is well done, you need not serve it that way—think pink for a change, and you'll soon find out how good lamb can taste!

Pork covers a multitude of cuts and curing techniques used for the meat of the hog. When buying fresh pork look for a grayish-pink to rose color, and again look for firm white fat. Cook fresh pork *at least* 30 minutes to the pound to be sure that no pink remains in the center of the meat. It's your best insurance to destroy any organisms that may be unhealthy for you, and to bring out the fullest flavor of the meat. A canned, fully cooked ham does not need any further cooking, unless you wish to bake it "Virginia style" or use it as the base of another cooked dish.

The following information helps you to decide what cut of meat to buy for what style of cooking, and then step by step tell you how to roast, broil, pan broil, braise, pan fry, and cook in liquid.

HOW TO COOK MEAT CORRECTLY

THE WAY TO ROAST:

1. Season with salt and pepper, if desired, or follow recipe directions.

2. Place meat fat side up on rack in open roasting pan.

3. Insert meat thermometer.

4. Do not cover. Do not baste.

5. Roast in slow oven of 300° F. to 350° F.

6. Roast to desired degree of doneness.

THE CUTS TO ROAST:

Beef:	Standing ribs, rolled ribs, rump of high quality, and ground beef loaf.
Veal:	Leg, loin, rack, shoulder (bone in), cushion-style shoulder, boned and rolled shoulder, ground veal loaf.
Pork:	Fresh or smoked loin, sirloin (bone in) or boneless sirloin, Boston shoulder, fresh or smoked picnic, fresh or smoked ham, smoked shoulder roll, spareribs, ground ham loaf.
Lamb:	Leg, shoulder (bone in), cushion-style shoulder, boned and rolled shoulder, ground lamb loaf.

THE WAY TO BROIL:

1. Set oven regulator for broiling.

2. Place meat 2 to 5 inches from heat.

3. Broil until top of meat is brown.

4. Season with salt and pepper, if desired, or follow recipe directions.

5. Turn meat and cook until done.

6. Season and serve at once.

THE CUTS TO BROIL:

Beef:	Rib, club, tenderloin (filet mignon), T-bone, porterhouse, tip, sirloin, and top round steaks; ground beef patties.
Pork:	Bacon, Canadian-style bacon, ham slices, sliced smoked shoulder roll, fresh or smoked chops.

Lamb:	Shoulder rib, loin, and sirloin chops; English lamb chops; steaks; ground lamb patties.
Variety Meats:	Sweetbreads, brains, veal or lamb liver, kidneys.

THE WAY TO PAN BROIL:

1. Place meat in heavy frying pan.

2. Do not add fat or water. Do not cover.

3. Cook slowly, turning occasionally.

4. Pour fat from pan as it accumulates.

5. Brown meat on both sides.

6. Season, if desired. Serve at once.

THE CUTS TO PAN BROIL:

Beef:	Rib, club, tenderloin (filet mignon), T-bone, porterhouse, tip, sirloin, and top round steaks; ground beef patties.
Smoked Pork:	Bacon, Canadian-style bacon, ham slices, sliced smoked shoulder roll, chops.
Lamb:	Shoulder, rib, loin, and sirloin chops; English lamb chops; steaks; ground lamb patties.
Variety Meats:	Sweetbreads; brains; veal, lamb liver; kidneys.

THE WAY TO BRAISE:

1. Brown meat on all sides in fat in heavy utensil.

2. Season with salt and pepper, if desired, or follow recipe directions.

3. Add small amount of liquid, if necessary.

4. Cover tightly.

5. Cook at low temperature until tender.

THE CUTS TO BRAISE:

Beef:	Pot roasts; arm, blade, round, and flank steaks; short ribs; plate; brisket; cross-cut shanks.

Veal:	Breast; steaks; rib, loin and kidney chops; cubes.
Pork:	Shoulder steaks, chops, spareribs, tenderloin, hocks.
Lamb:	Shoulder chops, breast, neck slices, shanks.
Variety Meats:	Heart, kidney, brains, liver, sweetbreads.

THE WAY TO PAN FRY:

1. Brown meat on both sides in small amount of fat.

2. Season with salt and pepper, if desired.

3. Do not cover.

4. Cook at moderate temperature until done, turning occasionally.

5. Remove from pan and serve at once.

THE CUTS TO PAN FRY:

Beef:	Thin rib, club, tenderloin (filet mignon), T-bone, porterhouse, sirloin and top round steaks; ground beef patties.
Veal:	Arm, shoulder, sirloin, and round steaks; rib, loin, and kidney chops.
Smoked Pork:	Ham slice, bacon, Canadian-style bacon, chops.
Lamb:	Shoulder, rib and loin chops; patties.
Variety Meats:	Sweetbreads; brains; liver; veal and lamb kidneys.

THE WAY TO COOK IN LIQUID:

1. Brown meat on all sides in own fat or lard, where desirable.

2. Season with salt and pepper, if desired, or follow recipe directions.

3. Cover with liquid, cover kettle, cook below boiling point until tender.

4. Add vegetables just long enough before serving to be cooked.

(Large cuts and stews)

Beef: Neck, shank, flank, heel of round, plate, brisket, short ribs, corned beef, stew meat.

Veal: Neck, breast, riblets, flank, shoulder, shank, heel of round, stew meat.

Smoked Pork: Ham, picnic, shoulder roll, shank.

Lamb: Neck, breast, riblets, flank, shank, stew meat.

Variety Meats: Heart, kidney, tongue, brains, sweetbreads.

SLICED SIRLOIN WITH ONIONS AND MUSHROOMS

To serve 2 or 3:	*To serve 4 to 6:*	
AMOUNT	AMOUNT	INGREDIENTS
1 (1 1/2 pound)	1 (3-pound)	Sirloin steak
1/4 teaspoon	1/2 teaspoon	Salt
1/8 teaspoon	1/4 teaspoon	Pepper
1 large	2 large	Onions, sliced thin
1/4 pound	1/2 pound	Fresh mushrooms, sliced
2 tablespoons	3 tablespoons	Butter
1 teaspoon	2 teaspoons	Bottled liquid gravy mix

Season steak with salt and pepper. Broil 5 minutes, then turn steak over and broil an additional 5 minutes, or until desired degree of doneness is achieved. Meanwhile, sauté sliced onion and mushrooms in butter until onions are translucent and tender. Stir in gravy mix and simmer until steak is done. Slice steak and cover it with onion-mushroom mixture. Serve at once.

If you are dining alone and want to treat yourself to a good steak, choose a well-trimmed porterhouse that weighs about a pound or more. Have the "tail" trimmed and ground, giving you a delicious hamburger patty for another meal. Spread the steak with prepared mustard to give it a tangy tenderness.

BROILED STEAK

For each serving:

AMOUNT	INGREDIENTS
1 (1-pound)	Porterhouse steak, trimmed, with "tail" ground into a patty.
1/2 teaspoon	Prepared mustard

Trim excess fat from steak to prevent a fat flareup in your broiler. Slash the fatty sides of the steak all around so it won't curl up during the broiling. Then spread the top of the steak with mustard. For a rare steak, broil about 7 minutes on each side; or until desired degree of doneness is reached. Salt and pepper as desired. Serve on a warm plate.

LONDON BROIL

To serve 2 or 3:	*To serve 4 to 6:*	
AMOUNT	AMOUNT	INGREDIENTS
1 (1-pound)	1 (2-pound)	Flank steak
1/4 teaspoon	1/2 teaspoon	Onion salt
1/4 teaspoon	1/2 teaspoon	Garlic salt
1/8 teaspoon	1/4 teaspoon	Black pepper
1 tablespoon	2 tablespoons	Melted butter

Place flank steak on a broiling pan. Combine onion salt, garlic salt, pepper, and melted butter. Brush top of steak with half of this mixture. Broil for 4 to 5 minutes. Turn steak over and brush with remaining mixture. Broil 4 minutes longer, or until steak is done to your taste. Carve meat into thin slices on an extreme diagonal across the grain. Serve at once.

You're having a few people in for dinner and you want to serve something that looks intricate but cooks without a lot of bother? Here's a Chinese-Stuffed Flank Steak that will do both. Easy on your pocketbook too!

CHINESE-STUFFED FLANK STEAK

To serve 4 to 6:

AMOUNT	INGREDIENTS
1 1/2 to 2 pounds	Flank steak
1 cup	Seasoned bread croutons
1	Egg, beaten
2 tablespoons	Chopped green onions
1/4 cup	Chopped onions
1 can (6-ounce)	Water chestnuts, chopped
1/4 teaspoon	Powdered poultry seasoning
1/2 teaspoon	Salt
1/4 teaspoon	Pepper
1 can (8-ounce)	Tomato sauce with mushrooms
2 tablespoons	Vegetable oil
1/2 cup	Beef bouillon
2 tablespoons	Vinegar
2 tablespoons	Sugar
1/2 teaspoon	Ginger
2 tablespoons	Soy sauce
2 tablespoons	Cornstarch

Score flank steak in a diamond pattern on one side. Combine croutons, egg, green onions, onion, water chestnuts, poultry seasoning, salt, pepper, and ¼ cup tomato sauce. Spread mixture evenly on unscored side of steak, leaving a 1-inch margin on each side. Roll up in jelly-roll fashion; secure with skewers. Brown on all sides in hot oil in a Dutch oven. Combine remaining tomato sauce, bouillon, vinegar, sugar, ginger, and soy sauce; add to meat and simmer for 1½ hours, covered. Remove flank steak with care, and place on a serving platter. Combine cornstarch with water and stir until smooth; spoon some sauce from the flank steak into the cornstarch mixture and then pour the mixture back in the Dutch oven to thicken the remaining sauce. Simmer and stir until sauce comes to a boil. Pour over flank steak and serve.

ROAST BEEF

To serve 3 or 4:	To serve 6 to 8:	
AMOUNT	AMOUNT	INGREDIENTS
2 1/2 pounds	4 pounds	Beef roast (sirloin tip, top sirloin, eye round)
1/4 teaspoon	1/2 teaspoon	Onion salt
1/4 teaspoon	1/2 teaspoon	Salt
1/8 teaspoon	1/4 teaspoon	Pepper
1/2 cup	1 cup	Water

Place beef roast in a flat open roasting pan; season with onion salt, salt, and pepper. Pour water in the bottom of the pan. Roast uncovered in a 325°F. oven for about 20 minutes to the pound if you like it rare in the center, 25 minutes to the pound for medium, and 27 to 30 minutes per pound if you like your beef well done. Remove from oven and set roast aside to "rest" for 10 minutes before carving; meanwhile, add boiling water to the pan and scrape the bottom to make a natural gravy. If the color is too pale, add a teaspoon of bottled liquid gravy mix for a fast pickup. Slice and serve.

Rib roast depends upon simple seasoning and superb timing to emerge prettily pink inside. Set your oven carefully and watch the clock to prevent overcooking.

RIB ROAST

To serve 4 to 6:	
AMOUNT	INGREDIENTS
1 (2-rib)	Beef roast
1/4 cup	Flour
1 teaspoon	Onion salt
1/2 teaspoon	Salt
1/4 teaspoon	Pepper
1 teaspoon	Paprika

Trim roast of excess fat, leaving a good covering of fat all around. Combine flour, onion salt, salt, pepper, and paprika until ingredients are well mixed. Pat roast all over with this mixture until it is completely coated with a fine dusting. Place roast in a flat pan, fat side up, resting on its bones. Roast in a 325°F. oven, about 20 minutes for each pound of roast to get rare meat; increase cooking time by 5 to 10 minutes per pound if you prefer it medium to well-done. When roast is cooked, remove it from the pan and let it "rest" about 10 minutes, making it easier to carve—cover it with a clean cloth (a dish towel is ideal) on top of the range. Then, for gravy, pour off most of the fat from the roasting pan and add a small amount of boiling water to the pan—scrape the fat residue into the water and stir. If the color is too pale, add a teaspoon or two of bottled liquid gravy and rescue it. Season with salt and pepper as desired.

SAUERBRATEN

| To serve 2 or 3: | To serve 4 to 6: | |
AMOUNT	AMOUNT	INGREDIENTS
2 1/2 pounds	4 pounds	Top round beef roast
1/2 teaspoon	3/4 teaspoon	Salt
1/8 teaspoon	1/4 teaspoon	Pepper
1 clove	1 clove	Garlic, peeled
1 cup	2 cups	Red wine vinegar
1/2 cup	1 cup	Water
2 tablespoons	1/4 cup	Sugar
1/4 cup	1/2 cup	Chopped onions
1	2	Bay leaves
3	6	Whole peppercorns
1 tablespoon	2 tablespoons	Flour
3 tablespoons	1/4 cup	Olive oil
4	8	Gingersnap cookies

Rub meat with salt, pepper, and cut side of garlic.

Place a large plastic bag in a deep bowl. Insert the beef roast, standing on end. Heat the wine vinegar, water, sugar, chopped onion, bay leaves and peppercorns together in a saucepan; do not boil, but rather simmer for about 5 minutes. Cool slightly. Pour this marinade over the beef roast and fasten the bag with a wire closure. Refrigerate for a day or two, turning the bag occasionally to redistribute the marinade. When ready to cook, remove meat and wipe it dry. Pat meat with flour. Heat oil in a Dutch oven; brown meat on all sides over high heat. Reduce heat, add remaining marinade, and simmer, covered, until meat is tender to the insertion of a fork, about 1½ to 2 hours. Remove meat, add crumbled gingersnaps to gravy, and simmer and stir until gravy thickens. Serve in thick slices smothered with gravy.

Like all pot roasts, this one requires long, slow cooking to make it fork-tender. Marinating is not necessary in this case—the wine and vinegar will accomplish their tenderizing and flavoring the 3- or 4-hour cooking period the pot roast requires.

CARDAMON POT ROAST

To serve 6 to 8:

AMOUNT	INGREDIENTS
4 to 5 pounds	Beef for pot roast (top or bottom round)
1/4 cup	Shortening
2 cups	Water
1 cup	Wine vinegar
1 cup	White dinner wine
1/2 cup	Brown sugar
1 cup	Chopped onions
2 tablespoons	Mixed pickling spice
2 teaspoons	Ground cardamon
1/3 cup	Sifted flour
1/3 cup	Water

Brown meat on all sides in heated shortening. Remove excess fat after browning. Add water, vinegar, wine, brown sugar, onion, pickling spice, and cardamon. Simmer, covered, about 3 to 4 hours or until meat is tender. Remove meat and keep warm. Strain gravy. Blend flour and ⅓ cup water together until smooth; stir into strained gravy. Cook, stirring until thickened. Serve over meat slices.

ONION-FLAVORED BRISKET

| To serve 2 or 3: | To serve 4 to 6: | |
AMOUNT	AMOUNT	INGREDIENTS
1 1/2 pounds	3 pounds	Fresh beef brisket, of the "first cut"
1/2 envelope	1 envelope	Dried onion soup mix
1/2 cup	1 cup	Water
1/2 teaspoon	1 teaspoon	Paprika

Arrange beef brisket in a flat roasting pan or Dutch oven. Sprinkle with onion soup mix, letting some fall in the pan around the beef. Add water to the pan. Sprinkle top of brisket with paprika. Cover tightly with foil or lid of Dutch oven. Bake in a low 300°F. oven for 60 minutes to the pound—making it 1½ hours for the smaller roast and 3 hours for the larger one. Add additional water to the gravy if it is needed. Meat should be tender and well done. Slice and serve with gravy.

EASY BEEF STROGANOFF

| To serve 2 or 3: | To serve 4 to 6: | |
AMOUNT	AMOUNT	INGREDIENTS
1 tablespoon	2 tablespoons	Flour
1 teaspoon	2 teaspoons	Salt
3/4 pound	1 1/2 pounds	Sirloin steak, cut in strips
2 tablespoons	1/4 cup	Butter
1 small	1 medium	Onion, sliced
1 clove	1 clove	Garlic, minced
1/2 can	1 can (10 3/4-ounce)	Condensed tomato soup
1/4 cup	1/2 cup	Water
1/8 teaspoon	1/4 teaspoon	Tabasco sauce
1/2 pound	1 pound	Mushrooms, sliced
1 1/2 cups	3 cups	Hot cooked rice
1/2 cup	1 cup	Dairy sour cream

Combine flour and salt; sprinkle meat with flour mixture. Melt butter in a skillet; add onion and garlic. Cook until onion is tender but not brown. Remove from skillet and set aside. Add meat to skillet and brown well on all sides. Return onion to the skillet; add soup, water, Tabasco, and sliced mushrooms. Cover; simmer over low heat for 30 minutes, or until meat is fork-tender. Stir in sour cream just before serving, being careful only to heat it through. Turn beef mixture into the center of a serving platter and spoon rice around the edge.

BEEF-VEGETABLE DELIGHT

To serve 2 or 3:	To serve 4 to 6:	
AMOUNT	AMOUNT	INGREDIENTS
3/4 pound	1 1/2 pounds	Boneless sirloin steak
1 teaspoon	2 teaspoons	Butter
1 package (10-ounce)	2 packages	Frozen Parisienne vegetables with sauce
1 teaspoon	2 teaspoons	Soy sauce
2 tablespoons	1/4 cup	Water

Slice steak into long, thin strips of bite-size pieces. Melt butter in a large skillet; quickly sear steak strips on all sides over high heat, stirring constantly. Turn heat low and add contents of the frozen package of vegetables. Add soy sauce and water; stir together and cover skillet tightly. Cook for 10 to 15 minutes over low heat, stirring occasionally until frozen squares of sauce are evenly distributed through the vegetables and meat. Serve at once on cooked rice, if desired.

Cook this Beef Bourguignonne the French way—covered and baked in the oven. It's a meal-in-one that can't be beat.

BEEF BOURGUIGNONNE

To serve 2 or 3:	*To serve 4 to 6:*	
AMOUNT	AMOUNT	INGREDIENTS
1 pound	2 pounds	Boned lean beef, cut into cubes
2 tablespoons	4 tablespoons	Flour
1/2 teaspoon	1 teaspoon	Paprika
1/4 teaspoon	1/2 teaspoon	Salt
1/8 teaspoon	1/4 teaspoon	Pepper
1 small clove	1 large clove	Garlic, minced
2 tablespoons	3 tablespoons	Olive oil
1/2 cup	1 cup	Burgundy wine
1 cup	2 cups	Bouillon
1 tablespoon	2 tablespoons	Tomato paste
6	12	Tiny white onions, peeled
1 small	1 large	Bay leaf
1/4 teaspoon	1/2 teaspoon	Thyme
3	6	Carrots, peeled and cut into chunks
3	6	Potatoes, peeled and cut into chunks
1/4 pound	1/2 pound	Mushrooms, sliced

Dredge beef chunks in combined flour, paprika, salt, and pepper. Add minced garlic to oil in a Dutch oven (heavy covered roasting pan) and heat; brown the beef chunks in this, turning carefully to sear all sides. Combine Burgundy wine, bouillon, and tomato paste; pour over meat. Arrange onions around the meat. Add bay leaf and thyme. Cover and bake in a 325°F. oven for 1½ to 2 hours. Then add chunks of carrots, potatoes, and sliced mushrooms; return to the oven for an additional 30 minutes or until the vegetables are tender. Remove bay leaf before serving.

Puchero is a South American-inspired dish that is a perfect meal-in-a-dish to serve a large group. It's the kind of adventurous cooking that will win olés every time.

PUCHERO

To serve 8:

AMOUNT	INGREDIENTS
2 pounds	Beef, chuck or bottom round, cut into large cubes
1/4 cup	Flour
2 1/2 teaspoons	Salt
1/4 teaspoon	Pepper
3 tablespoons	Salad oil
3 medium	Onions, sliced
5 cups	Water
1	Bay leaf
1 (3- to 3 1/2-pound)	Broiler chicken, cut up
2 tablespoons	Chopped parsley
6	Carrots, scraped, cut into 1-inch pieces
4 ears	Corn, cut in halves (or 2 10-ounce packages frozen corn)
8	Small whole zucchini squash (or 4 medium ones), cut in halves
2 cans (20-ounces each)	Garbanzos or chick-peas, drained
6	Bananas, cut in halves

Roll beef cubes in mixture of flour, ½ teaspoon of the salt, and all the pepper; brown in hot oil in a Dutch oven or large heavy kettle. Add onions and brown well. Add water and bay leaf and bring to a boil. Simmer, covered, for 1 hour. Add chicken and remaining 2 teaspoons salt and simmer, covered, for 1 hour more. Add parsley, carrots, corn, garbanzos, and zucchini; continue to simmer, covered, 30 minutes, or until meat and vegetables are tender. Add additional water if needed. Add bananas, and cook, covered, 10 minutes longer. Serve hot in soup plates with broth spooned over.

WALNUT MEAT LOAF

To serve 2 or 3:	To serve 4 to 6:	
AMOUNT	AMOUNT	INGREDIENTS
1 pound	2 pounds	Ground beef
1/2 cup	1 cup	Chopped walnuts
1/4 cup	1/2 cup	Uncooked oatmeal
1	2	Eggs, beaten
1/4 cup	1/2 cup	Water
2 tablespoons	1/4 cup	Dried onion flakes
3/4 teaspoon	1 1/2 teaspoons	Salt
1/2 teaspoon	1 teaspoon	Worcestershire sauce
1/8 teaspoon	1/4 teaspoon	Pepper

Place ground beef, chopped walnuts, and oatmeal in a bowl. Add water to beaten egg and pour this mixture into beef; mix everything together. Add onion flakes, salt, Worcestershire sauce, and pepper; mix thoroughly. Pack the mixture into a loaf pan and bake at 350°F. for 1 hour for smaller loaf and 1 hour and 20 minutes for the larger loaf. Remove loaf from oven and let stand in pan for 5 minutes; drain off fat. Slice and serve.

The ingredients for this flavorful meat loaf should be combined several hours, even overnight, before baking, to give the fullest taste possible. Even the leftovers will taste delicious!

MARINATED MEAT LOAF

To serve 2 or 3:	To serve 4 to 6:	
AMOUNT	AMOUNT	INGREDIENTS
3/4 pound	1 1/2 pounds	Ground lean beef
1	1	Egg, beaten
1/4 cup	3/4 cup	Milk
1 cup	2 cups	Soft bread crumbs
1/3 cup	2/3 cup	White dinner wine
2 tablespoons	1/4 cup	Finely chopped onion
1/2 teaspoon	1 teaspoon	Celery salt

To serve 2 or 3:	To serve 4 to 6:	
AMOUNT	AMOUNT	INGREDIENTS
1/2 teaspoon	1 teaspoon	Salt
1/2 teaspoon	1 teaspoon	Mustard
1 tablespoon	2 tablespoons	Chopped dill pickle
3/4 cup	1 1/2 cups	Grated American cheese

Combine ground beef with beaten egg and milk. Add bread crumbs, wine, and remaining ingredients; mix until well blended. Cover and refrigerate several hours to blend flavors. Pack mixture into a lightly greased loaf pan. Bake in a 350°F. oven for 1 to 1½ hours.

PIZZA LOAF

To serve 2 or 3:	To serve 4 to 6:	
AMOUNT	AMOUNT	INGREDIENTS
1	2	Eggs
1/2 can	1 can (10 1/2-ounce)	Pizza sauce
3/4 teaspoon	1 1/2 teaspoons	Salt
1/8 teaspoon	1/4 teaspoon	Pepper
1 cup	2 cups	Corn Flakes
1 pound	2 pounds	Lean ground beef
2 tablespoons	1/4 cup	Finely chopped onion
1/3 cup	2/3 cup	Canned mushrooms, stems and pieces
4 slices	4 slices	Mozzarella cheese

Place eggs, pizza sauce, salt, pepper, and Corn Flakes in a large mixing bowl; beat until thoroughly combined. Add ground beef, onion, and mushrooms; mix thoroughly. Spread ½ of meat mixture in ungreased square baking pan. Place 2 slices of cheese over meat mixture. Spread remaining meat mixture evenly over cheese. Bake in a 350°F. oven for 1 hour, or until meat starts to shrink from sides of pan. Meanwhile, cut remaining cheese into narrow strips. Remove meat from oven, arrange cheese in lattice strips diagonally over top of loaf. Return to oven and continue baking about 3 minutes longer, or until cheese is slightly melted. Cut into squares.

MONTERREY CASSEROLE

To serve 2 or 3:	To serve 4 to 6:	
AMOUNT	AMOUNT	INGREDIENTS
1/2 pound	1 pound	Ground lean beef
1 tablespoon	2 tablespoons	Chopped onion
1/4 teaspoon	1/2 teaspoon	Seasoned salt
1 can (8-ounce)	2 cans	Tomato sauce
1 cup	2 cups	Grated Cheddar cheese
2 cups	4 cups	Taco-flavored tortilla chips
1/4 cup	1/2 cup	Ripe olives (black)

Cook beef in a skillet for 5 minutes, until crumbly and light in color, breaking it up with a fork as it cooks. Add onion, salt, and tomato sauce. Simmer for 5 minutes. Place ¾ of the tortilla chips in a casserole; sprinkle ½ of the grated cheese over the chips. Pour meat sauce over and top with remaining grated cheese. Garnish with remaining tortilla chips. Bake in a 350°F. oven for 15 minutes. Top with ripe olives before serving.

SKILLET CABBAGE ROLLS

To serve 2 or 3:	To serve 4 to 6:	
AMOUNT	AMOUNT	INGREDIENTS
6	12	Large cabbage leaves
1/2 pound	1 pound	Ground beef
3/4 cup	1 1/2 cups	Packaged stuffing mix
1/2 cup	1 cup	Finely chopped onion
1/2 cup	1 cup	Shredded mozzarella or Swiss cheese
1 can (8-ounce)	2 cans	Tomato sauce with cheese
2 tablespoons	1/4 cup	Water
3/4 teaspoon	1 1/2 teaspoons	Salt
1/8 teaspoon	1/4 teaspoon	Pepper

Place cabbage leaves in boiling water; let stand until limp. Remove leaves from water and drain. Mix ground beef, stuffing mix, ½ of the onion, the shredded cheese, and 4 tablespoons of the tomato sauce. Divide meat mixture equally among cabbage leaves. Roll leaves around the meat mixture, starting at the stem end—cover ball of meat with stem end of cabbage, fold sides inward over stem end, and roll toward top edge of leaf. (Fasten with toothpicks or place outer fold down in the skillet.) Mix remaining tomato sauce, remaining onion, water, salt, and pepper in a skillet. Heat to boiling. Place cabbage rolls in sauce; reduce heat to simmer over low heat. Cook, covered, for 1 hour, basting occasionally.

PARMESAN MEATBALLS WITH MUSHROOM SAUCE

To serve 2 or 3:	*To serve 4 to 6:*	
AMOUNT	AMOUNT	INGREDIENTS
1/2 pound	1 pound	Lean ground beef
1	1	Egg
3 tablespoons	1/4 cup	Fine soft bread crumbs
1 tablespoon	2 tablespoons	Grated Parmesan cheese
1/2 teaspoon	1 teaspoon	Salt
1 tablespoon	2 tablespoons	Butter
1/2 can	1 can (10 1/2-ounce)	Condensed cream of mushroom soup
2 tablespoons	1/4 cup	Sherry wine
2 tablespoons	1/4 cup	Water
1 tablespoon	2 tablespoons	Chopped parsley

Combine beef, egg, crumbs, cheese, and salt. Take up mixture by rounded teaspoonfuls and shape into balls. Melt butter in a large, heavy skillet; add meatballs and brown on all sides. Blend mushroom soup, sherry, water, and parsley; pour over meatballs. Cover and simmer for 20 minutes. Stir occasionally during cooking, and add a little more water if sauce seems too thick. Serve with noodles, rice, or mashed potatoes.

MEATBALL SKILLET

To serve 2 or 3:	*To serve 4 to 6:*	
AMOUNT (MEATBALLS)	AMOUNT (MEATBALLS)	INGREDIENTS
1/2 pound	1 pound	Ground beef
1/2 cup	1 cup	Soft bread crumbs
1/3 cup	3/4 cup	Instant nonfat dry milk
2 tablespoons	1/4 cup	Chopped onion
1	1	Egg, slightly beaten
2 tablespoons	1/4 cup	Water
1/4 teaspoon	1/2 teaspoon	Salt
Dash	1/8 teaspoon	Pepper
AMOUNT (SAUCE)	AMOUNT (SAUCE)	
2 tablespoons	4 tablespoons	Butter
1 tablespoon	2 tablespoons	Chopped onion
1 1/2 tablespoons	3 tablespoons	Flour
1/4 teaspoon	1/2 teaspoon	Salt
3/4 cup	1 1/2 cups	Water
1/4 cup	1/2 cup	Instant nonfat dry milk
1/2 cube	1 cube	Beef bouillon
1 jar (2-ounce)	1 jar (4-ounce)	Mushrooms, undrained

In a bowl lightly mix beef, crumbs, dry milk, onion, egg, water, salt,
and pepper just until blended. Shape mixture into meatballs, about
2 inches in diameter. In a large covered skillet melt butter; brown
meatballs slowly on all sides. Remove meatballs from skillet and set
aside on warm platter.

For the sauce: Sauté onion in butter until tender; stir in flour and
salt. Remove from heat; gradually stir water, and then dry milk. Add
bouillon cube and mushrooms. Cook over medium heat until thickened, stirring constantly. Return meatballs to skillet, cover, and
simmer for 15 minutes.

BEEF AND RICE CASSEROLE

To serve 2 or 3:	*To serve 4 to 6:*	
AMOUNT	AMOUNT	INGREDIENTS
2 tablespoons	2 tablespoons	Butter
1/4 cup	1/4 cup	Finely chopped onion
1/4 cup	1/4 cup	Chopped green pepper
1/2 pound	1 pound	Ground beef

| To serve 2 or 3: | To serve 4 to 6: | |
AMOUNT	AMOUNT	INGREDIENTS
1/2 teaspoon	1 teaspoon	Salt
2 tablespoons	1/4 cup	Unsulphured molasses
1 tablespoon	2 tablespoons	Prepared mustard
1 cup	2 cups	Canned tomatoes
1/2 cup	1 cup	Raw rice

Melt butter in a large skillet; add onion and green pepper and cook until onion is tender but not brown. Add ground beef and ½ of the salt. Brown beef, breaking it up into pieces with a fork as it cooks. While the beef is browning, combine molasses and prepared mustard. Add to beef mixture with tomatoes and remaining salt. Gradually add rice. Cover; reduce heat and simmer 25 to 30 minutes, or until rice is tender. If you use quick-cooking rice, reduce simmering time to 10 minutes, or until rice is tender.

HOT CHILI POT

To serve 12:

AMOUNT	INGREDIENTS
6 tablespoons	Butter
5 medium	Onions, sliced
3 pounds	Ground beef
2 tablespoons	Chili powder
1 tablespoon	Salt
1 teaspoon	Paprika
3/4 teaspoon	Tabasco sauce
2 cans (1 pound, 12 ounces each)	Tomatoes
1 can (6-ounce)	Tomato paste
3 cans (20 ounces each)	Kidney beans

Melt butter in a 6- to 8-quart saucepan. Add onion and cook until tender and translucent, but not brown. Add beef; sprinkle with chili powder, salt, paprika, and Tabasco. Cook meat until brown, breaking up with a fork. Add tomatoes and tomato paste; cover and simmer 45 minutes. Add kidney beans; simmer 15 minutes longer. Serve hot. Chili may be frozen after cooling to room temperature; to reheat, let thaw at room temperature about 2 hours before heating.

Liver is highly nutritious and economical as well. Here's an easy way to make it taste delicious. Serve it with hot buttered noodles and a crisp salad.

LIVER STROGANOFF

To serve 2 or 3:	To serve 4 to 6:	
AMOUNT	AMOUNT	INGREDIENTS
1/4 pound	1/2 pound	Sliced bacon
1	2	Onions, sliced
1/4 pound	1/2 pound	Mushrooms, sliced
1 pound	2 pounds	Beef or calf's liver, cut into strips
2 tablespoons	1/4 cup	Flour
1/2 cup	1 cup	Milk
1/4 teaspoon	1/2 teaspoon	Tabasco sauce
1/4 teaspoon	1/2 teaspoon	Powdered dried thyme
1/4 teaspoon	1/2 teaspoon	Salt
1/2 cup	1 cup	Dairy sour cream

Fry bacon until crisp. Remove from skillet and drain off all but 4 tablespoons of the drippings. Add onions and mushrooms; cook until tender. Remove and set aside. Toss liver with ¾ of the flour (1½ tablespoons for the 2-to-3 amount, 3 tablespoons for the 4-to-6 amount) until liver strips are well coated with the flour. Add to skillet and cook 5 to 7 minutes, stirring frequently. Add onions and mushrooms. Blend remaining flour with milk, Tabasco, thyme, and salt. Add to liver mixture; cook, stirring constantly, until mixture thickens and comes to a boil. Stir in sour cream; heat but do not boil. Serve at once, garnished with bacon slices.

LEFTOVER MEAT CASSEROLE

To serve 2 or 3:	To serve 4 to 6:	
AMOUNT	AMOUNT	INGREDIENTS
1 1/2 cups	3 cups	Diced cooked meat
1/4 teaspoon	1/2 teaspoon	Salt
1/8 teaspoon	1/4 teaspoon	Tabasco sauce
1 can (1-pound)	2 cans	Zucchini and tomatoes

To serve 2 or 3:	To serve 4 to 6:	
AMOUNT	AMOUNT	INGREDIENTS
1 can (1-pound)	2 cans	Whole white onions, drained
1 package (10-ounce)	2 packages	Frozen peas and carrots, thawed
1 1/2 cups	3 cups	Mashed potatoes (may be made from instant dried potatoes, if desired)

Place meat in middle of large ovenproof skillet or casserole. Combine salt and Tabasco with zucchini and tomatoes; add to skillet with drained onions. Sprinkle peas and carrots over vegetables. Prepare mashed potatoes (as directed on package if you are using instant mashed potatoes). Spoon potatoes around the edge of the casserole. Bake in a 400°F. oven for about 15 minutes, or until potatoes are lightly browned.

VEAL MARSALA

To serve 2 or 3:	To serve 4 to 6:	
AMOUNT	AMOUNT	INGREDIENTS
3/4 pound	1 1/2 pounds	Thin veal slices
1/2 teaspoon	1 teaspoon	Salt
1/4 teaspoon	1/2 teaspoon	Pepper
1 tablespoon	2 tablespoons	Flour
1/4 cup	1/2 cup	Olive oil
1/4 pound	1/2 pound	Sliced fresh mushrooms (canned mushrooms may be substituted; a 4-ounce can will serve 2 or 3; an 8-ounce can, 4 to 6)
1/2 cup	1 cup	Marsala wine

Flatten veal slices with a meat mallet or with the broad side of a knife. Combine salt, pepper, and flour; dredge veal slices in this mixture until all are lightly coated. Heat oil in a skillet; brown veal slices on both sides, doing several at a time and removing them when browned to make room for the remaining slices. When you have removed the last slices, sauté the mushrooms in the remaining oil, adding additional oil if necessary. Then return the veal slices to the skillet; pour Marsala wine over all, and cook for 5 minutes longer. Serve at once.

VEAL PARMIGIANA

To serve 2 or 3:	*To serve 4 to 6:*	
AMOUNT	AMOUNT	INGREDIENTS
3/4 pound	1 1/2 pounds	Thin veal slices
1/2 teaspoon	1 teaspoon	Salt
1/4 teaspoon	1/2 teaspoon	Pepper
1 tablespoon	2 tablespoons	Flour
1/4 cup	1/2 cup	Olive oil
6 thin slices	12 thin slices	Mozzarella cheese
1 cup	2 cups	Canned spaghetti sauce
2 tablespoons	4 tablespoons	Parmesan cheese

Flatten veal slices with a meat mallet or with the broad side of a knife. Combine salt, pepper, and flour; dredge veal slices in this mixture until all are lightly coated. Heat oil in a skillet; brown veal slices on both sides. Place them in a flat baking dish when browned. Top each veal slice with slices of mozzarella cheese, pour spaghetti sauce over all and top with a sprinkling of Parmesan cheese. Bake in a 350°F. oven for 20 minutes, or until cheese is melted. Serve at once.

SALTIMBOCCA

To serve 2 or 3:	*To serve 4 to 6:*	
AMOUNT	AMOUNT	INGREDIENTS
1 pound	2 pounds	Veal round steak
2 tablespoons	1/4 cup	Chopped parsley
3 ounces	6 ounces	Sliced ham
2 tablespoons	3 tablespoons	Vegetable oil
1 can (8-ounce)	2 cans	Tomato sauce with cheese

Pound veal steak to ¼ inch thick; pound in parsley. Lay slices of ham over veal and roll up jelly-roll style; fasten with toothpicks. Brown veal roll in oil in a skillet. Pour tomato sauce over; cover and simmer over low heat for 1 hour, or until tender.

VEAL STEW WITH CHEESE GRAVY

To serve 2 or 3:	To serve 4 to 6:	
AMOUNT	AMOUNT	INGREDIENTS
1 1/2 tablespoons	3 tablespoons	Flour
1/4 teaspoon	1/2 teaspoon	Salt
3/4 pound	1 1/2 pound	Boneless veal, cut into strips
1 1/2 tablespoons	3 tablespoons	Butter
1 cup	2 cups	Water
2	4	Potatoes, peeled and cut into eighths
2	4	Carrots, peeled and cut into 1-inch pieces
1/2 cup	1 cup	Sliced onions
1/4 teaspoon	1/2 teaspoon	Salt
6 tablespoons	3/4 cup	Instant nonfat dry milk
1/2 tablespoon	1 tablespoon	Flour
1/4 cup	1/2 cup	Water
1/4 cup	1/2 cup	Grated Parmesan cheese

Combine flour and first listing of salt; coat meat with the mixture. In a large covered skillet melt butter; brown meat on all sides. Add first listing of water; cover and simmer 45 minutes or until meat is almost tender. Add potatoes, carrots, and onions; sprinkle with second listing of salt. Cook 30 minutes, or until vegetables are tender. In a small bowl combine nonfat dry milk and flour; gradually stir in second listing of water until smooth. Gradually add this mixture to the skillet. Cook, stirring constantly, until liquid is thickened; cook 2 additional minutes; stir in Parmesan cheese. Serve at once.

BARBECUED LAMB RIBLETS

To serve 2 or 3: AMOUNT	To serve 4 to 6: AMOUNT	INGREDIENTS
1 1/2 pounds	3 pounds	Lamb riblets
1/4 cup	1/2 cup	Dijon-style prepared mustard
2 tablespoons	1/4 cup	Honey
1/2 teaspoon	1 teaspoon	Crushed rosemary leaf
1/2 clove	1 clove	Garlic, crushed
1/4 teaspoon	1/2 teaspoon	Salt

Place riblets on a rack in a shallow roasting pan. Bake in a 325°F. oven for about 1½ hours; drain off drippings. Combine mustard, honey, rosemary, garlic, and salt; brush mixture over ribs. Bake 30 to 40 additional minutes turning ribs and basting with additional sauce several times.

SAVORY SHOULDER LAMB CHOPS

To serve 2 or 3: AMOUNT	To serve 4 to 6: AMOUNT	INGREDIENTS
3	6	Shoulder lamb chops
1/4 cup	1/2 cup	Bouillon
1/4 cup	1/2 cup	Dry white wine
1 small	1 medium	Onion, sliced
2 tablespoons	1/4 cup	Chopped parsley
1 1/2 teaspoons	1 tablespoon	Cornstarch
2 tablespoons	1/4 cup	Water

In a large skillet, brown chops on both sides; drain off drippings. Add bouillon, wine, onion, and parsley; simmer, covered, 45 minutes or until lamb is tender. Blend cornstarch with water; stir into pan and cook, stirring constantly, for a minute or so until sauce is boiling. Garnish with parsley, if desired.

SKILLET LAMB CHOPS WITH ORANGE SAUCE

To serve 2: AMOUNT	To serve 4: AMOUNT	INGREDIENTS
1 tablespoon	2 tablespoons	Butter
2	4	Shoulder lamb chops, 3/4-inch thick
1/4 teaspoon	1/2 teaspoon	Salt
1/8 teaspoon	1/4 teaspoon	Pepper
1 1/2 teaspoons	1 tablespoon	Grated orange rind
1/4 cup	1/2 cup	Orange juice
1 1/2 teaspoons	1 tablespoon	Lemon juice
1/8 teaspoon	1/4 teaspoon	Curry powder
1 1/2 teaspoons	1 tablespoon	Cornstarch
2 tablespoons	1/4 cup	Water
1	2	Large navel oranges, peeled and sectioned

In a large covered skillet melt butter; brown chops on both sides; season with salt and pepper. Add orange rind and juice, lemon juice, and curry powder. Cover and simmer over low heat for 45 minutes or until tender. Remove chops and keep warm. Add sufficient water to drippings to make 1 cup; combine cornstarch with water and gradually add to skillet. Cook over medium heat, stirring constantly, until mixture thickens. Cook 2 additional minutes. Add orange sections and heat to serving temperature (do not boil). Pour sauce over chops and serve.

GLAZED SHISH KEBAB

To serve 2 or 3: AMOUNT	To serve 4 to 6: AMOUNT	INGREDIENTS
1 cup	2 cups	Currant jelly
3 tablespoons	6 tablespoons	Lime juice
2 tablespoons	1/4 cup	Butter
1/2 teaspoon	1 teaspoon	Salt
1/8 teaspoon	1/4 teaspoon	Pepper
1/8 teaspoon	1/4 teaspoon	Nutmeg
3/4 pound	1 1/2 pounds	Lean lamb cubes
1/4 teaspoon	1/2 teaspoon	Salt
1/8 teaspoon	1/4 teaspoon	Pepper
6 large	12 large	Fresh mushrooms

Mix together currant jelly, lime juice, butter, salt and pepper (first listings) and nutmeg; heat, stirring, until butter is melted and glaze is smooth. Place lamb on skewers, season with salt and pepper (second listings) and place mushrooms on the end of each skewer. Brush with glaze. Broil 10 minutes on each side, brushing frequently with additional glaze. Serve with remaining glaze.

For an interesting departure from the traditional Shish Kebab, try Stew-on-a-Skewer. It is simmered and then threaded on serving skewers with zucchini and carrots—to be served nestled in a bed of fluffy rice.

STEW-ON-A-SKEWER

To serve 2 or 3:	To serve 4 to 6:	
AMOUNT	AMOUNT	INGREDIENTS
1 pound	2 pounds	Boneless lamb
1 tablespoon	2 tablespoons	Flour
1/2 teaspoon	1 teaspoon	Garlic salt
1 teaspoon	2 teaspoons	Paprika
Dash	1/8 teaspoon	Pepper
1/4 teaspoon	1/2 teaspoon	Dried rosemary
1 1/2 tablespoons	3 tablespoons	Shortening
1/3 cup	2/3 cup	Sauterne (or other white wine)
1 1/2 teaspoons	1 tablespoon	Wine vinegar
2/3 cup	1 1/3 cups	Bouillon
2 small	4 small	Carrots
2 small	4 small	Zucchini
1 for each skewer	1 for each skewer	Spiced crabapples

Trim any excess fat from meat; cut meat into chunks about 1½ inches in diameter. Mix together flour, salt, paprika, pepper, and rosemary. Roll meat in seasoned flour; brown slowly on all sides in heated shortening. Sprinkle any flour remaining from dredging over meat; add wine, vinegar, and bouillon. Cover tightly and simmer over low heat until meat is tender, about 1½ hours. Just before meat is done, pare carrots and cut ends from zucchini; cut vegetables into generous chunks and cook in boiling salted water until tender-crisp. Drain and season with a little melted butter, salt, and pepper. Skim any excess fat from the pan gravy; thicken slightly, if desired, with a little cornstarch mixed with cold water. Thread chunks of meat and vegetable on long serving skewers with a crab-apple at the end for garnish. Arrange on a bed of hot cooked rice. Serve gravy separately.

LAMB STROGANOFF

| To serve 2 or 3: | To serve 4 to 6: | |
AMOUNT	AMOUNT	INGREDIENTS
2 tablespoons	1/4 cup	Flour
1/2 teaspoon	1 teaspoon	Salt
1/8 teaspoon	1/4 teaspoon	Pepper
3/4 pound	1 1/2 pounds	Boneless lamb shoulder, thinly sliced
2 tablespoons	4 tablespoons	Butter
1 clove	1 clove	Garlic, minced
1 tablespoon	2 tablespoons	Butter
1/4 pound	1/2 pound	Sliced mushrooms
1/4 cup	1/2 cup	Chopped onions
2 tablespoons	1/4 cup	Tomato sauce
2 tablespoons	1/4 cup	Water
1/2 teaspoon	1 teaspoon	Caraway seed
1/2 package	1 package (3-ounce)	Cream cheese, softened
1/2 cup	1 cup	Dairy sour cream

Combine flour, salt, and pepper; coat meat with this mixture. In a large heavy covered skillet, melt the first listing of butter. Add garlic and meat; brown meat slowly, tossing occasionally to brown on all sides. Remove meat from skillet and add the second listing of butter to the skillet. Add mushrooms and onions; sauté 3 to 5 minutes. Return meat to skillet; stir in tomato sauce, water, and caraway seed. Cover and simmer for 15 to 20 minutes, or until meat is tender. Blend in cream cheese (which has been left at room temperature for about ten minutes), then sour cream just before serving; do not boil, just heat to serving temperature. Serve at once over rice or noodles.

LAMB PEPPER STEAK

To serve 2 to 3:	To serve 4 to 6:	
AMOUNT	AMOUNT	INGREDIENTS
3/4 pound	1 1/2 pounds	Lean boneless lamb shoulder, cut into 1/2-inch strips
2 tablespoons	4 tablespoons	Butter
1/8 teaspoon	1/4 teaspoon	Garlic powder
1/4 cup	1/2 cup	Chopped onions
1/2 cup	1 cup	Water
1	2	Green peppers, cut into strips
2 tablespoons	1/4 cup	Water
1 tablespoon	2 tablespoons	Cornstarch
1 1/2 tablespoons	3 tablespoons	Soy sauce
1/2 teaspoon	1 teaspoon	Salt
1/8 teaspoon	1/4 teaspoon	Pepper

In a large skillet with cover, melt butter; stir in garlic powder and onion. Add meat strips and brown slowly on all sides. Add first listing of water and cover; simmer 20 minutes, or until meat is fork-tender. Add peppers and simmer an additional 10 minutes. Combine second listing of water with cornstarch, soy sauce, salt, and pepper; stir until smooth. Stir into meat mixture. Cook, stirring constantly, until thickened. Cook 2 additional minutes. Serve over rice, if desired.

LAMB LOAF

To serve 2 or 3:	To serve 4 to 6:	
AMOUNT	AMOUNT	INGREDIENTS
1 pound	2 pounds	Ground lamb
1/4 cup	1/2 cup	Chopped onion
2 tablespoons	1/4 cup	Chopped green pepper
1/4 cup	1/2 cup	Fine dry bread crumbs
1/2 can	1 can (8-ounce)	Tomato sauce
1	2	Eggs, slightly beaten
1/2 teaspoon	1 teaspoon	Salt
1/8 teaspoon	1/4 teaspoon	Pepper

To serve 2 or 3:	To serve 4 to 6:	
AMOUNT	AMOUNT	INGREDIENTS
1/8 teaspoon	1/4 teaspoon	Crushed rosemary leaf
1 slice	2 slices	Bacon

In a large bowl combine lamb, onion, green pepper, crumbs, tomato sauce, eggs, salt, pepper, and rosemary. Shape into a loaf in a baking pan. Cut bacon into pieces and lay across top of loaf. Bake in a preheated 350°F. oven for 45 minutes to 1 hour. Let stand 10 minutes before serving.

BARBECUED SPARERIBS

To serve 2 or 3:	To serve 4 to 6:	
AMOUNT	AMOUNT	INGREDIENTS
2 1/2 pounds	5 pounds	Spareribs (pork)
2 tablespoons	1/4 cup	Butter
1/3 cup	2/3 cup	Chopped onion
2 tablespoons	1/4 cup	Light brown sugar
1 teaspoon	2 teaspoons	Salt
1 teaspoon	2 teaspoons	Chili powder
1/2 teaspoon	1 teaspoon	Dry mustard
1/2 cup	1 cup	Pineapple juice
1/4 cup	1/2 cup	Lemon juice
1/2 cup	1 cup	Catsup
1/4 cup	1/2 cup	Chili sauce
1 1/2 teaspoons	1 tablespoon	Soy sauce
2 drops	4 drops	Tabasco sauce

Cut ribs in 2- or 3-rib portions. Place in shallow roasting pan, meaty side up; roast uncovered in preheated 350°F. oven for 1 hour. Meanwhile, in a saucepan, melt butter; sauté onion in butter until tender. Blend in sugar, salt, chili powder, and mustard. Stir in pineapple and lemon juices, catsup, chili, soy, and Tabasco sauces. Heat to boiling; reduce heat and simmer 30 minutes. Place ribs under broiler and spoon sauce over ribs. Broil for 20 minutes, turning and basting with sauce frequently.

Plan to prepare this recipe when you have at least 3 hours to spare before dining. It's well worth the effort for the flavor of the orange is baked right in for a tangy taste. A brand new way to serve pork and beans!

ORANGE RIB 'N' BEAN BAKE

To serve 3 to 4:

AMOUNT	INGREDIENTS
3 pounds	Spareribs, cut into 2-rib pieces
1/2 teaspoon	Salt
1/4 teaspoon	Pepper
2 tablespoons	Butter
1	Onion, chopped
1 cup	Orange juice
1/4 cup	Soy sauce
2 tablespoons	Lemon juice
1 teaspoon	Thyme, crushed
1	Orange, unpeeled, thinly sliced
1	Lemon, unpeeled, thinly sliced
2 packages (10-ounce)	Frozen lima beans

Sprinkle ribs with salt and pepper; place in a shallow roasting pan. Bake at 475°F. for 30 minutes, turning once. Meanwhile, sauté onion in butter until tender but not brown. Add orange juice, soy sauce, lemon juice, and thyme. Bring to a boil. Drain excess fat from browned ribs; place a slice of orange and lemon on each rib, add warm sauce. Reduce heat to 350°F.; bake, covered, an additional 2¼ hours. Add lima beans during the last 1¼ hours of baking.

PORK CHOP 'N' BEAN BAKE

To serve 3:	*To serve 6:*	
AMOUNT	AMOUNT	INGREDIENTS
3	6	Pork chops
1 can (21-ounce)	2 cans	Pork and beans
2 tablespoons	1/4 cup	Dry onion soup mix
2 tablespoons	1/4 cup	Brown sugar
1 tablespoon	2 tablespoons	Prepared mustard
1/4 cup	1/2 cup	Catsup

Brown chops in a skillet. Meanwhile, place pork and beans and remaining ingredients in a flat baking dish. Mix well; nestle chops in bean mixture. Bake, covered, at 350°F. for 30 to 35 minutes.

PORK CHOP–SWEET POTATO CASSEROLE

| *To serve 2 or 3:* | *To serve 4 to 6:* | |
AMOUNT	AMOUNT	INGREDIENTS
3	6	Sweet potatoes
3	6	Pork chops
2 tablespoons	1/4 cup	Unsulphured molasses
2 tablespoons	1/4 cup	Water
1/2 teaspoon	1 teaspoon	Instant minced onion
1/8 teaspoon	1/4 teaspoon	Dry mustard
1/8 teaspoon	1/4 teaspoon	Ginger
1/2 teaspoon	3/4 teaspoon	Salt

Cook sweet potatoes in boiling salted water for 15 minutes. Drain, cool slightly, peel, and cut in half. Arrange potato halves in a greased casserole. Brown chops slowly on both sides in a skillet for 15 to 20 minutes. Combine molasses, water, instant minced onion, dry mustard, and ginger; pour over sweet potatoes. Sprinkle pork chops on both sides with salt; arrange over sweet potatoes. Bake, covered, in a 350°F. oven for 1 hour, or until chops are tender. Serve with Cherry Sauce, below, if desired.

CHERRY SAUCE

| *To serve 2 or 3:* | *To serve 4 to 6:* | |
AMOUNT	AMOUNT	INGREDIENTS
1/2 can	1 can (1 pound)	Tart pitted cherries, water-packed
1/4 cup	1/2 cup	Sugar
1 tablespoon	2 tablespoons	Cornstarch
1/8 teaspoon	1/4 teaspoon	Salt
1/8 teaspoon	1/4 teaspoon	Dry mustard

To serve 2 or 3:	To serve 4 to 6:	
AMOUNT	AMOUNT	INGREDIENTS
1/8 teaspoon	1/4 teaspoon	Ginger
A few drops	A few drops	Red food coloring
1 1/2 teaspoons	1 tablespoon	Butter

Drain liquid from cherries into a measuring cup; add water to make ¾ cup liquid for the 2-to-3 amount, and 1½ cups liquid for the 4-to-6 amount. Combine sugar, cornstarch, salt, dry mustard, and ginger in a saucepan; gradually blend in liquid. Stir constantly over moderate heat until the mixture thickens and comes to a boil. Add cherries and a few drops of red food coloring to make a rich red color. Cook 3 more minutes; remove from heat and stir in butter. Serve in a sauceboat or little pitcher along with Pork Chop–Sweet Potato Casserole (above).

BAKED VIRGINIA HAM

To bake a 5- to 7-pound ham:

AMOUNT	INGREDIENTS
1	Fully cooked canned ham
1/4 cup	Whole cloves
1 cup	Pineapple juice
1 tablespoon	Brown sugar

Open can and remove ham to a roasting pan. Score top of ham with crossing diagonal lines, forming 1-inch diamonds; stud corners of these diamonds with whole cloves pressed into the meat. Stir together the pineapple juice and brown sugar; Spoon over the top of the ham. Bake in a 325°F. oven for about 1 hour. Remove from oven and serve, or refrigerate until serving time.

APPLE AND HAM PANCAKES

To serve 2 or 3:	To serve 4 to 6:	
AMOUNT	AMOUNT	INGREDIENTS
1 cup	2 cups	Canned apple sauce
1/4 cup	1/2 cup	Light brown sugar
1/4 teaspoon	1/2 teaspoon	Cinnamon
1/8 teaspoon	1/4 teaspoon	Allspice
1 tablespoon	2 tablespoons	Butter
1/4 teaspoon	1/2 teaspoon	Grated lemon rind
1 1/2 teaspoons	1 tablespoon	Lemon juice
1 cup	2 cups	Pancake mix
1/4 pound	1/2 pound	Boiled ham, sliced thin

Combine apple sauce, sugar, cinnamon, allspice, butter, lemon rind, and juice. Simmer 5 minutes; keep hot until ready to serve. Prepare pancakes according to directions on package. Place ham slice betwen two griddle cakes; top with apple sauce mixture. Serve immediately.

HAM-MACARONI SALAD

To serve 2 or 3:	To serve 4 to 6:	
AMOUNT	AMOUNT	INGREDIENTS
1/2 cup	1 cup	Uncooked macaroni
1 cup	2 cups	Diced cooked ham
2 tablespoons	1/4 cup	Diced sweet pickles (or pickle relish)
1 tablespoon	2 tablespoons	Chopped pimiento
1 teaspoon	2 teaspoons	Grated onion
1/2 can	1 can (8-ounce)	Tomato sauce
1/4 cup	1/2 cup	Mayonnaise
1 1/2 ounces	3 ounces	Softened cream cheese
1 teaspoon	2 teaspoons	Prepared mustard
1/8 teaspoon	1/4 teaspoon	Salt
2	4	Hard-cooked eggs, quartered

Cook macaroni in salted water until tender; drain and cool. Combine macaroni with ham, pickles, pimiento, and onion. Blend together tomato sauce, mayonnaise, cream cheese (which has been allowed to soften at room temperature for 10 minutes) mustard, and salt; combine with the macaroni mixture. Chill. Serve on salad greens, garnished with quartered eggs.

ORANGE-GLAZED HAM BALLS

To serve 2 or 3:	To serve 4 to 6:	
AMOUNT	AMOUNT	INGREDIENTS
3/4 pound	1 1/2 pounds	Ground cooked ham
1/2 cup	1 cup	Oatmeal
1	2	Eggs, beaten
1 1/2 teaspoons	1 tablespoon	Brown sugar
Dash	1/8 teaspoon	Ground cloves
Dash	1/8 teaspoon	Nutmeg
3 tablespoons	1/3 cup	Cooking oil
1/4 cup	1/2 cup	Brown sugar
2 teaspoons	4 teaspoons	Cornstarch
1 teaspoon	2 teaspoons	Fresh grated orange peel
1/2 cup	1 cup	Orange juice
1/2 cup	1 cup	Water
2 tablespoons	1/4 cup	Lemon juice
1	2	Oranges, peeled, cut into bite-size pieces

Thoroughly combine ham, oatmeal, beaten egg, brown sugar (first listing), cloves, and nutmeg. Shape into balls and chill. Lightly brown ham balls in hot oil. Drain off excess oil before adding sauce.

To make sauce: Thoroughly combine sugar and cornstarch. Blend in orange peel and juice gradually until smooth; add water and lemon juice. Pour mixture over ham balls. Cook about 45 minutes over low heat. Gently stir in orange pieces; heat until warm, then serve.

LEFTOVER HAM LOAF

To serve 2 or 3:	To serve 4 to 6:	
AMOUNT	AMOUNT	INGREDIENTS
2/3 cup	1 1/3 cups	Water
1/8 teaspoon	1/4 teaspoon	Salt
2/3 cup	1 1/3 cups	Minute rice
1 1/2 cups	3 cups	Ground cooked ham
2 tablespoons	1/4 cup	Finely chopped onion
1	2	Eggs
1/2 can	1 can (10 1/2-ounce)	Condensed cream of mushroom soup
1 package (9-ounce)	2 packages	Italian green beans (frozen)
3 tablespoons	1/3 cup	Milk

Bring water and salt to a boil. Stir in rice. Cover; remove from heat, and let stand for 5 minutes. Then add ham and onion to prepared rice. Combine eggs and ⅓ of the condensed soup. Add to rice mixture; toss lightly until it is well mixed. Spoon into a greased loaf pan; pack down lightly. Cover with aluminum foil. Bake at 350°F. for 45 minutes. Let stand about 5 minutes; then invert. Add milk to remaining condensed soup, heat, and pour over loaf. Spoon cooked beans around the loaf. Serve hot.

FRANKFURTER CASSEROLE

To serve 2 or 3:	To serve 4 to 6:	
AMOUNT	AMOUNT	INGREDIENTS
3	6	Frankfurters
1/2 cup	1 cup	Corn chips
1/2 cup	1 cup	Canned tomatoes, drained
1 tablespoon	2 tablespoons	Chopped green pepper
1 tablespoon	2 tablespoons	Chopped onion
1/2 cup	1 cup	Canned (or frozen) whole kernel corn
1/2 teaspoon	1 teaspoon	Salt
1/2 teaspoon	1 teaspoon	Chili powder
1	2	Eggs

Slice frankfurters and place in a greased casserole. Add corn chips, tomatoes, pepper, onion, corn, salt, chili powder, and eggs. Mix through. Bake at 350°F. for 40 minutes. Serve hot.

CALCUTTA CURRY

To serve 2 or 3:	*To serve 4 to 6:*	
AMOUNT	AMOUNT	INGREDIENTS
1 can (12-ounce)	2 cans	Luncheon meat
2 1/2 cups	5 cups	Cooked rice
3 tablespoons	6 tablespoons	Butter
1 can (1-pound)	2 cans	Mixed fruits for salad
1 tablespoon	1 1/2 to 2 tablespoons	Curry powder
1/4 teaspoon	1/2 teaspoon	Ginger
1 1/2 teaspoons	1 tablespoon	Prepared mustard
2 teaspoons	4 teaspoons	Cornstarch
1/4 cup	1/2 cup	Water
1/4 cup	1/2 cup	Chopped peanuts (optional)
1/4 cup	1/2 cup	Raisins (optional)
1/4 cup	1/2 cup	Grated coconut (optional)

Prepare rice according to package directions. Set aside and keep warm. Open can of luncheon meat and cut into quarters lengthwise and then cut each quarter into seven lengthwise slices. Set aside. Drain the contents of the can of fruit, reserving the syrup. In a saucepan, melt the butter and add curry powder, ginger, and prepared mustard. Stir until well blended, then add the reserved fruit syrup and heat until bubbling. Mix the cornstarch in the water until smooth, then add to fruit-syrup mixture. Add the luncheon meat strips and drained fruit. Continue to cook over low heat for about 6 minutes, stirring occasionally. Serve over hot fluffy white rice. Have small dishes of peanuts, raisins, and grated coconut to spoon over all, if desired.

SAUSAGES AND RICE

To serve 2 or 3:	To serve 4 to 6:	
AMOUNT	AMOUNT	INGREDIENTS
1/2 pound	1 pound	Link pork sausages, cut up
1 small	1 medium	Onion, cut in wedges
1/2	1	Green pepper, cut up
2/3 cup	1 1/3 cups	Minute rice
1	1	Chicken bouillon cube
2/3 cup	1 1/3 cups	Hot water

Sauté sausages in hot skillet until well browned. Remove sausages; keep warm. Sauté onion and green pepper in the drippings. Stir in rice. Cook over low heat, stirring constantly, for 3 to 4 minutes or until slightly browned. Meanwhile, dissolve bouillon cube in hot water. Add to mixture in skillet; bring quickly to a full boil. Add sausages. Cover and remove from heat. Let stand 5 minutes or until most of the liquid is absorbed. Serve at once.

10 · Poultry Tricks

You can juggle a budget to your benefit if you include several poultry meals a week in your menu planning. Besides being economical, high in nutrition, and low in calories, poultry is also adaptable to a variety of cooking techniques.

Remember to remove the plastic wrappings from your package of poultry before refrigerating it, and then to cook it as soon as possible. After cooking, it will keep fresh for several days in the refrigerator, and the leftovers are a bonanza for soups, salads, and casseroles.

After seasoning poultry, cook it "low and slow" for best results. "High and fast" gives you a tough bird.

Most ready-to-cook poultry is at least partially cleaned. But remove any remaining pinfeathers and wash away any clinging interior particles. Rub a cut half of lemon over the surfaces, both inside and out, to remove any offending odor. Then season and cook according to the recipe directions.

Frozen poultry may be cooked without thawing, if it has been cleaned before freezing. It is easier to handle if it is in parts. If the bird has been frozen whole, immerse it in a watertight wrapper in cold water, until the giblets are pliable enough to be removed. Once thawed, cook the poultry promptly. Stuff just before roasting, and remove stuffing to a separate bowl before storing leftovers in the refrigerator—if the stuffing is left in the bird for storage the cold may not penetrate the bird to the center cavity and there is danger of bacteria growth that will cause illness.

When choosing a turkey for roasting, keep in mind that the bone structure stops growing at about the 10-pound size, so every pound over that is proportionately more meat and less bone for the price. You don't need a special occasion to cook a small boneless turkey roast, and they are available in all-white-meat form if that is your preference.

Here's a roasting guide to help you determine how long your poultry selection should cook in the oven:

KIND OF POULTRY	WEIGHT	ROASTING TIME (AT 325°F.)
Chickens	1 1/2 to 2 1/4 lbs.	1 to 2 hrs.
	2 1/2 to 4 1/2 lbs.	2 to 3 1/2 hrs.
Ducks	4 to 6 lbs.	2 to 3 hrs.
Turkeys	6 to 8 lbs.	3 to 3 1/2 hrs.
	8 to 12 lbs.	3 1/2 to 4 1/2 hrs.
	12 to 16 lbs.	4 1/2 to 5 1/2 hrs.
	16 to 20 lbs.	5 1/2 to 6 1/2 hrs.
	20 to 24 lbs.	6 1/2 to 7 hrs.

SIMPLE BAKED CHICKEN

To serve 2 or 3:	To serve 4 to 6:	
AMOUNT	AMOUNT	INGREDIENTS
1	2	Broiler chickens, quartered
2 tablespoons	1/4 cup	Softened butter
1/2 teaspoon	1 teaspoon	Salt
1/4 teaspoon	1/2 teaspoon	Pepper
1/4 teaspoon	1/2 teaspoon	Tarragon
1/2 cup	1 cup	Water

Rub chicken with butter on both sides; sprinkle with salt, pepper, and tarragon. Place quarters, skin side down, in a shallow baking pan. Bake in a moderate 375°F. oven for 30 minutes. Turn chicken; add water. Bake 20 minutes longer.

CHICKEN PAPRIKA

To serve 2 or 3:	To serve 4 to 6:	
AMOUNT	AMOUNT	INGREDIENTS
1	2	Broiler chickens, cut up
1/2 teaspoon	1 teaspoon	Monosodium glutamate (optional)
1 teaspoon	2 teaspoons	Salt
1 1/2 teaspoons	1 tablespoon	Paprika
3/4 cup	1 1/4 cups	Water
1/4 cup	1/3 cup	Finely chopped onion
1/2 cup	1 cup	Dairy sour cream
1/2 package	1 package (8-ounce)	Wide noodles

Sprinkle chicken with monosodium glutamate, ½ of the salt, and ½ of the paprika. Place under broiler heat for 10 minutes or until browned, turning once. Then put chicken pieces in a large skillet; add water and chopped onion. Cover; simmer over low heat for 40 minutes. Remove chicken to serving platter. Add remaining salt and paprika, and sour cream to the mixture in the skillet. Heat just to serving temperature, stirring constantly; do not boil or mixture will have a curdled appearance. Spoon sauce over chicken. Serve with wide noodles, cooked according to package directions.

BAKED CHICKEN WITH SPAGHETTI

To serve 2 or 3:	To serve 4 to 6:	
AMOUNT	AMOUNT	INGREDIENTS
3/4 cup	1 1/2 cups	Corn flake crumbs
3/4 teaspoon	1 1/2 teaspoons	Salt
1/4 teaspoon	1/3 teaspoon	Pepper

To serve 2 or 3:	To serve 4 to 6:	
AMOUNT	AMOUNT	INGREDIENTS
3	6	Chicken drumsticks
3	6	Chicken thighs
1/3 cup	2/3 cup	Evaporated milk
1 can (1 pound)	2 cans	Marinara sauce
8 ounces	1 pound	Uncooked spaghetti

Combine corn flake crumbs with salt and pepper in a shallow dish. Line shallow baking pan with aluminum foil. Dip chicken parts in evaporated milk, then roll immediately in seasoned corn flake crumbs. Place chicken in foil-lined pan. Bake in a 350°F. oven for 1 hour, or until tender. No need to cover or turn chicken while baking. Meanwhile, cook spaghetti according to package directions. Heat marinara sauce. Spoon sauce over drained spaghetti on a large serving platter; top with chicken pieces.

CHICKEN CORDON BLEU

To serve 2:	To serve 4:	
AMOUNT	AMOUNT	INGREDIENTS
1	2	Whole chicken breasts, boned, skinned, and split in half
2	4	Thin slices cooked ham
2	4	Thin slices mozzarella cheese
2 teaspoons	4 teaspoons	Grated Parmesan cheese
1/3 cup	2/3 cup	Corn flake crumbs
1/4 teaspoon	1/2 teaspoon	Salt
Dash	1/8 teaspoon	Pepper
3 tablespoons	1/3 cup	Melted butter

Pound each half of chicken breast as thin as possible, without tearing flesh. Place 1 ham slice and 1 cheese slice in center of each chicken piece; sprinkle each with 1 teaspoon Parmesan cheese. Bring 4 corners of chicken pieces to center, overlapping edges so ham and cheese are completely enclosed. Press to seal. Combine corn flake crumbs (if you don't have a package of crumbs, crush regular corn flakes and then measure), salt, and pepper in a shallow pan. Dip chicken pieces in melted butter; then coat evenly with crumbs mixture. Place chicken pieces in single layer, overlapped edges down, in a greased shallow baking pan. Bake at 350°F. about 25 minutes, or until chicken is tender.

OVEN-FRIED CHICKEN

| To serve 2 or 3: | To serve 4 to 6: | |
AMOUNT	AMOUNT	INGREDIENTS
3 tablespoons	1/3 cup	Butter
3	6	Chicken drumsticks
3	6	Chicken thighs
1 teaspoon	2 teaspoons	Salt
1/3 cup	2/3 cup	Flour
2 tablespoons	1/4 cup	Grated Parmesan cheese
1/4 teaspoon	1/2 teaspoon	Paprika
1/4 teaspoon	1/2 teaspoon	Oregano
1/4 cup	1/2 cup	Milk

Place butter in a foil-lined baking pan; put in a hot 425°F. oven until butter melts, about 5 minutes. Sprinkle ½ of the salt over both sides of the chicken pieces. Combine the remaining salt with flour, grated cheese, paprika, and oregano. Dip chicken pieces in milk; then roll in the flour mixture. Place skin side down in melted butter. Bake for 25 minutes; turn and bake 20 minutes longer.

CHICKEN STEW

| To serve 2 or 3: | To serve 4 to 6: | |
AMOUNT	AMOUNT	INGREDIENTS
1	2	Broiler chickens, cut up
3 cups	6 cups	Water
1 1/2 teaspoons	1 tablespoon	Salt
1 teaspoon	2 teaspoons	Monosodium glutamate (optional)
1/8 teaspoon	1/4 teaspoon	Pepper
1	2	Bay leaf

To serve 2 or 3:	To serve 4 to 6:	
AMOUNT	AMOUNT	INGREDIENTS
1/2 cup	1 cup	Chopped celery
1 package (10-ounce)	2 packages	Frozen peas
3	6	Carrots, pared and quartered
6	12	Small white onions
5 tablespoons	10 tablespoons	Flour
3 tablespoons	6 tablespoons	Water

Place chicken in a deep kettle. Add water, salt, monosodium gluta-mate, pepper, bay leaf, and celery. Cover, and bring to a boil; reduce heat and simmer for 30 minutes. Add peas, carrots, and onions; simmer for 20 to 30 minutes more. Blend flour and water to a smooth paste; blend in a small amount of hot broth from the kettle of chicken; return this mixture to the kettle, stirring constantly as you bring it to a boil to thicken. Remove bay leaf before serving.

CHICKEN AND FRUIT SALAD

To serve 2 or 3:	To serve 4 to 6:	
AMOUNT	AMOUNT	INGREDIENTS
1	2	Whole chicken breasts
1/2 teaspoon	1 teaspoon	Salt
2 cups	4 cups	Water
1/4 cup	1/2 cup	Mayonnaise
1 tablespoon	2 tablespoons	Dairy sour cream
1/2 teaspoon	1 teaspoon	Lemon juice
1/8 teaspoon	1/4 teaspoon	Nutmeg
Dash	1/8 teaspoon	Curry powder
1 can (1-pound)	2 cans	Fruit cocktail, drained
2 tablespoons	1/4 cup	Slivered almonds

Combine chicken, salt, and water in a saucepan and simmer for about 35 minutes, until chicken is fork-tender. Meanwhile, mix to-gether the mayonnaise, sour cream, lemon juice, nutmeg, and curry powder. When chicken is tender and still warm remove bones, and cut into ½-inch cubes. Add dressing mixture and toss lightly until all chicken is coated. Chill for 30 minutes. When ready to serve, add well-drained fruit cocktail and slivered almonds. Toss lightly; serve on crisp lettuce leaves.

PINEAPPLE-CHEESE CHICKEN

To serve 2 or 3: AMOUNT	To serve 4 to 6: AMOUNT	INGREDIENTS
1 (2 1/2-pound)	2 (2 1/2-pound)	Broiler chickens, cut up
1/4 cup	1/2 cup	Flour
1 teaspoon	2 teaspoons	Salt
1/4 teaspoon	1/2 teaspoon	Pepper
1/4 teaspoon	1/2 teaspoon	Ground thyme
3 tablespoons	6 tablespoons	Butter
1 can (8 3/4-ounce)	1 can (1-pound)	Pineapple tidbits, drained
1/4 cup	1/2 cup	Pineapple syrup from drained tidbits
1 can (2-ounce)	1 can (4-ounce)	Sliced mushrooms, undrained
1/2 cup	1 cup	Shredded Cheddar cheese

In a clean paper bag combine flour, salt, pepper, and thyme. Add chicken pieces, one at a time, and shake to coat evenly. In a large skillet melt butter; brown chicken. Meanwhile, drain pineapple, reserving syrup. Place chicken in a flat baking pan. Top with mushrooms and liquid, then pineapple tidbits and amount of reserved pineapple syrup listed. Bake in a 350°F. oven for 40 minutes; remove from oven and top chicken pieces with cheese. Return to oven; bake an additional 10 minutes. Serve at once.

ORANGE BARBECUED CHICKEN

To serve 2 or 3: AMOUNT	To serve 4 to 6: AMOUNT	INGREDIENTS
1/4 cup	1/2 cup	Butter
2 tablespoons	1/4 cup	Orange marmalade
1 tablespoon	2 tablespoons	Lemon juice
1/4 teaspoon	1/2 teaspoon	Ground ginger
1	2	Broiler chickens, cut up
1/4 teaspoon	1/2 teaspoon	Salt
1/8 teaspoon	1/4 teaspoon	Pepper

In a small saucepan melt butter; add orange marmalade, lemon juice, and ground ginger. Simmer and stir for 2 or 3 minutes. Season chicken with salt and pepper; place on a pan, flesh side up. Brush ¼ of the marmalade mixture on the chicken; broil for 15 minutes, then turn chicken to skin side and brush with marmalade every 5 minutes until done, about 15 minutes.

Leftover chicken can take a starring role with this Chicken Creole casserole. Serve it over hot broad noodles for an easy and complete dinner.

CHICKEN CREOLE

| *To serve 2 or 3:* | *To serve 4 to 6:* | |
AMOUNT	AMOUNT	INGREDIENTS
2 tablespoons	4 tablespoons	Butter
1/2 cup	1 cup	Chopped onions
1/4 cup	1/2 cup	Chopped celery
1/4 cup	1/2 cup	Chopped green pepper
1/2 can	1 can (1-pound)	Tomatoes
1/2 teaspoon	1 teaspoon	Salt
1/2 teaspoon	1 teaspoon	Chili powder
Dash	1/8 teaspoon	Pepper
1/4 cup	1/2 cup	Instant nonfat dry milk
1 tablespoon	2 tablespoons	Flour
1/4 cup	1/2 cup	Water
1 cup	2 cups	Diced cooked chicken
1/2 cup	1 cup	Shredded Cheddar cheese

In a saucepan, melt butter; sauté onion, celery, and green pepper until tender. Add tomatoes, salt, chili powder, and pepper; cover and simmer 15 minutes. Meanwhile, in a small bowl combine nonfat dry milk and flour; gradually stir in water until smooth. Gradually add milk mixture to tomato sauce; cook over medium heat, stirring constantly, until thickened. Cook 2 additional minutes. Add chicken; cover and heat over low heat, stirring occasionally. Add cheese; stir until melted. Serve over noodles, if desired.

CREAMED CHICKEN ON WAFFLES

To serve 2 or 3:	*To serve 4 to 6:*	
AMOUNT	AMOUNT	INGREDIENTS
1/2 can	1 can (4-ounce)	Sliced mushrooms
1/2 cube	1 cube	Chicken bouillon
1 1/2 tablespoons	3 tablespoons	Butter
1/2 tablespoon	1 tablespoon	Instant minced onion
1/8 cup	1/4 cup	Chopped green pepper
1 1/2 tablespoons	3 tablespoons	Flour
Dash	1/8 teaspoon	Ground allspice
1/4 teaspoon	1/2 teaspoon	Salt
Dash	1/8 teaspoon	Pepper
1 scant cup	1 2/3 cups	Canned evaporated milk
1 cup	2 cups	Cut up cooked (or canned) chicken
1 tablespoon	2 tablespoons	Chopped pimiento
2 or 3	4 to 6	Frozen waffles

Drain and measure liquid from mushrooms. If necessary, add water to make ¼ cup liquid for the 2-to-3 recipe, and enough to make ½ cup liquid for the 4-to-6 recipe. Heat liquid; add bouillon cube and stir to dissolve. In medium-size saucepan, melt butter over low heat. Add drained mushrooms, onion, and green pepper; cook until pepper is tender, about 2 or 3 minutes. Remove from heat. Sprinkle in flour a little at a time, blending smoothly. Add allspice, salt, and pepper. Stir in mushroom liquid and evaporated milk. Cook and stir over medium heat until thickened. Add chicken and pimiento; heat to serving temperature. Serve over heated waffles.

ROAST TURKEY

To serve 6 to 8:

AMOUNT	INGREDIENTS
1 (12-pound)	Turkey
1/2 cup	Melted butter
1/2 teaspoon	Garlic powder
1/2 teaspoon	Salt
1 teaspoon	Paprika
1 teaspoon	Soy sauce

Clean, rinse, and pat turkey dry. Rub salt on interior and exterior surfaces. Place in a large roasting pan. Combine melted butter, garlic powder, salt, paprika, and soy sauce; paint the entire exterior surface with ½ this mixture. Cover top of turkey loosely with a large piece of aluminum foil; remove this foil during last hour, for browning. Roast in a 325°F. oven for 4 hours, or until turkey leg moves easily when jiggled. Baste several times with remaining butter mixture. When finished, remove from oven and let turkey "rest" for 20 minutes before carving.

PINEAPPLE-GLAZED TURKEY ROLL

To serve 6 to 8:

AMOUNT	INGREDIENTS
1 (4- to 6-pound)	Turkey roll
2 tablespoons	Brown sugar
1 tablespoon	Cornstarch
1 can (8-ounce)	Crushed pineapple
2 tablespoons	Soy sauce
1/4 teaspoon	Ginger

Arrange turkey roll in a roasting pan. In a small saucepan, combine sugar and cornstarch; stir in juice drained from crushed pineapple. Heat until thickened; add soy sauce, ginger, and drained pineapple. Spoon over turkey roll, covering the surface as much as possible. Place in a 350°F. oven and bake for 2 to 2 ½ hours. Slice and serve.

If you're tired of eating leftover turkey but don't know how to prepare it in an interesting way, here's a cheese-flavored casserole that will be a treat. Perhaps you'll deliberately make a larger turkey to be sure there are leftovers—and don't hesitate to substitute leftover chicken.

TURKEY SALAD BAKE

To serve 2 or 3:	*To serve 4 to 6:*	
AMOUNT	AMOUNT	INGREDIENTS
1 cup	2 cups	Shredded Cheddar cheese
2 cups	4 cups	Cut-up cooked turkey
3/4 cup	1 1/2 cups	Chopped celery
2 tablespoons	1/4 cup	Finely chopped green pepper
1 tablespoon	2 tablespoons	Chopped onions
1/2 cup	1 cup	Dairy sour cream
2 tablespoons	1/4 cup	Flour
1 tablespoon	2 tablespoons	Lemon juice
1/4 teaspoon	1/2 teaspoon	Salt
Dash	1/8 teaspoon	Pepper
1 cup	2 cups	Corn chips

Set aside 2 tablespoons Cheddar cheese for the 2-to-3 recipe, and ¼ cup for the 4-to-6 recipe. In a large bowl, combine remaining cheese, turkey, celery, green pepper, and onion. Blend together sour cream and flour; stir in lemon juice, salt, and pepper. Toss sour cream mixture lightly with turkey. Turn into a shallow casserole. Garnish with reserved cheese and corn chips. Bake in a preheated 350°F. oven for 20 minutes. Serve at once.

ORIENTAL TURKEY

| To serve 2 or 3: | To serve 4 to 6: | |
AMOUNT	AMOUNT	INGREDIENTS
1 1/2 cups	3 cups	Diced cooked turkey (or chicken)
1/3 cup	2/3 cups	Diced onions
1/2	1	Green pepper, sliced
2 tablespoons	3 tablespoons	Vegetable oil
1 can (6-ounce)	2 cans	Water chestnuts, drained and sliced
1 1/2 cans (8-ounce size)	3 cans	Tomato sauce with mushrooms
1/3 cup	2/3 cup	Water
1/4 teaspoon	1/2 teaspoon	Salt
Dash	1/8 teaspoon	Pepper
1 1/2 cups	3 cups	Crisp Chinese noodles

Lightly brown turkey, onion, and green pepper in oil in a large skillet. Add water chestnuts, tomato sauce, water, salt, and pepper. Simmer 20 minutes. Serve over Chinese noodles.

CHICKEN LIVERS MANDARIN

| To serve 2 or 3: | To serve 4 to 6: | |
AMOUNT	AMOUNT	INGREDIENTS
1 pound	2 pounds	Chicken livers
1 large	2 large	Onions, sliced thin
1 1/2 tablespoons	3 tablespoons	Butter
1/4 cup	1/2 cup	Flour
1/4 teaspoon	1/2 teaspoon	Salt
1 can (2-ounce)	1 can (4-ounce)	Button mushrooms
1 can (8-ounce)	1 can (1-pound)	Mandarin oranges
1 teaspoon	2 teaspoons	Cornstarch
1 tablespoon	2 tablespoons	Brown sugar
1 tablespoon	2 tablespoons	Soy sauce

Rinse chicken livers and discard any attached hearts; cut away any green parts as they will be bitter. Sauté onions in butter until translucent. Combine flour and salt; dredge livers in this sauté the livers with the onions about 4 minutes on each side. Pour in mushrooms, including juice. In a small saucepan, combine juice from Mandarin oranges, cornstarch, brown sugar, and soy sauce; cook until thickened. Add drained orange segments to the chicken livers and pour soy sauce mixture over all; stir to blend. Serve at once with fluffy rice.

ROCK CORNISH HEN

To serve 1 or 2:

AMOUNT	INGREDIENTS
1 (12- to 24-ounce)	Rock Cornish hen (under 1 pound will serve 1 person, 1 1/2 pound size will serve 2)
1/2	Lemon
1/2 teaspoon	Salt
1/4 teaspoon	Pepper
1 tablespoon	Melted butter
2 tablespoons	Orange marmalade

Rinse and dry hen. Rub inside and out with the ½ lemon; tuck this piece of lemon into the cavity of the hen, remembering to remove it before serving. Salt and pepper exterior of hen; brush with melted butter. Bake in a 350°F. oven for 45 minutes to 1 hour, depending on size. Paint surface with orange marmalade about 15 minutes before hen is done. Serve at once.

QUICK AND EASY RICE STUFFING

Prepare a package of convenience food mix of wild and white rice, following directions on the package. Or heat the boil-in-the-bag frozen package of wild and white rice. When the hens are done, spoon the hot rice mixture into the cavities and serve. To prevent a slippery messy time, prop each hen cavity-side up in a small deep bowl or pot. Then use two spoons—one to scoop up the rice mixture and the other to push it off the first spoon into the hen's cavity. Don't pack it down tight, just fill it up!

ROAST DUCK

To serve 4:

AMOUNT	INGREDIENTS
1 (5-pound)	Duck
1/2	Lemon
1 clove	Garlic
1/2 teaspoon	Salt
1/4 teaspoon	Pepper
1	Orange, quartered
1/2 cup	Seedless raisins
1 cup	Orange juice

Rinse and dry duck. Rub inside and out with cut lemon. Rub inside and out with garlic clove. Salt and pepper all surfaces. Tuck lemon, quartered orange, and raisins into the duck cavity, remembering to remove and discard it all before serving. Brush orange juice over the skin, and continue to baste with the orange juice during roasting. Roast uncovered in a 325°F. oven for 1 ½ hours. Quarter and serve.

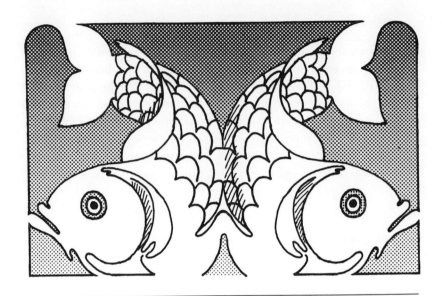

11 · Fish Finesse

If you have ever baited a hook and then had to cope with the catch, you will appreciate the efficient array of fish products on the market today. You can choose from frozen prepared fish of every origin, from already breaded shrimp to neat fillets of lemon sole. Ready-to-eat canned fish includes tuna, salmon, sardines, herring, and shellfish. And fresh fish is available cleaned and scaled.

You'll need one-third to one-half pound of fish per person of dressed fish, and one pound per person of whole fish that has to be trimmed of its scales, entrails, head, fins, and tail. The first rule when cooking fish: be gentle. Poach it rather than boil it. Don't overcook it if you want to be rewarded with memorable meals.

The following information will help you to recognize the different forms in which fresh and frozen fish are available. It will tell you what pre-preparations they need and the best ways to cook them. Following that are directions for the actual cooking techniques that will enable you to eat seafood at its peak of tastiness.

FISH PRIMER

Form	Definition	Pre-Preparation	Best Ways to Cook
Whole, fresh	Just as it comes from the water	Have scales and entrails removed. Head, fins, and tail may be removed. Cook whole, or cut into serving-size pieces	Bake, poach, broil, fry, steam
Drawn, fresh or frozen	Whole fish, eviscerated	Scale. Head, fins, and tail may be removed. Cook whole or in serving-size pieces	Bake, poach, broil, fry, steam
Dressed, fresh or frozen	Ready to cook	Cut into steaks or fillets	Bake, poach, broil, fry, steam
Steaks, fresh and frozen	Cross-section cuts or large fish	None	Bake, poach, broil, fry, steam
Fillets, fresh and frozen	Meaty sides of the fish, usually boned	None	Bake, poach, broil, fry, steam
Breaded Fillets, frozen	Fillet with seasoned crumb coating	None	Oven fry, deep fry
Breaded Portions frozen	Uniform serving portions cut from frozen blocks of popular fish. Seasoned crumb coating	None	Oven fry, deep fry
Fish Sticks, frozen	Uniform sticks, cut from frozen fillet blocks. Seasoned crumb coating	None	Oven fry, deep fry
Green, fresh or frozen	Raw, in-shell shrimps	Remove shell and black vein in back, before or after simmering	Simmer, bake, broil, pan fry, oven fry
Peeled, fresh or	Shrimp from which shell has	Remove black sand vein	Simmer, bake, broil, pan fry,

Form	Definition	Pre-Preparation	Best Ways to Cook
frozen	been removed		oven fry
Deveined	Peeled shrimp from which the black sand has been removed	None	Simmer, bake, broil, pan fry oven fry
Shucked, fresh or frozen	Removed from shell. Used to describe oysters, clams, and mussels	Wash out sand and bits of shell. If frozen, thaw before cooking	Steam, bake, sauté
Tail, fresh or frozen	Meat from the tail of the spiny lobster, usually sold in the shell	None	Bake, broil, or simmer

HOW TO BAKE: Place steaks, fillets, or whole fish in a greased baking dish. Brush with seasoned butter, and bake in a preheated oven at approximately 350°F. or at the temperature suggested in the recipe. Stuff whole fish with an herb and bread stuffing, or marinate fish before baking. For frozen fish, follow package directions.

HOW TO BROIL: Arrange steaks, fillets, or whole fish on a preheated, well-greased broiler rack. Brush with melted butter or basting sauce. For steaks and fillets, place rack about 2 inches from heat; for whole or split fish, place rack 3 to 6 inches from heat. Fillets and split fish do not need to be turned. Turn steaks and whole fish once, basting again, to broil second side. Serve immediately.

HOW TO PAN FRY: This method is usually reserved for small whole fish such as trout. Other forms such as fillets, steaks, and drawn fish may be pan fried although broiling is generally preferred. Bread the fish by dipping first in milk, then into bread crumbs. Use melted shortening or vegetable oil to cover bottom of pan ⅛ inch deep. Fry fish until light brown, turn, and brown other side. Too high a temperature will cause fat to smoke. Serve on hot platter.

HOW TO OVEN FRY: This is the method most often used to

cook frozen breaded fillets, sticks, or portions. Place the breaded fish in a shallow, lightly greased pan or on a baking sheet and bake according to package directions.

HOW TO DEEP FRY: Use a deep, heavy 3-quart saucepan and fill halfway with oil or melted vegetable shortening. Heat slowly until 375°F., using a thermometer to check temperature. Frying at too low a temperature causes foods to soak up shortening; at too high a temperature, shortening will smoke and cause disagreeable odors and flavors. Place fish in bottom of the fryer basket or on a large slotted spoon and lower into pan. Fry until golden brown; drain and serve immediately. Allow shortening to return to 375°F. before adding a second batch.

HOW TO POACH: Place fish on a flat, greased tray of a poacher or on a strip of greased heavy-duty foil or in cheesecloth. Lower into pan and cover with seasoned liquid or wine. Simmer gently until fish is cooked and remove from liquid. The liquid in which the fish is poached might be a fish stock, court bouillon, or wine that may be used as the base for sauce for the fish.

HOW TO STEAM: Steaming is much like poaching, except that the fish is placed over the liquid. Place fish in a deep pan on a greased perforated rack or tray that will hold it above liquid level. Bring liquid to a boil and cover pan tightly. Cook until done. Season and salt fish after steaming. Liquid used in steaming can be the base for sauce for the fish.

FILLETS OF SOLE WITH CLAM SAUCE

To serve 2 or 3:	To serve 4 to 6:	
AMOUNT	AMOUNT	INGREDIENTS
1 pound	2 pounds	Fillet of sole
2 tablespoons	1/4 cup	Flour
2 tablespoons	1/4 cup	Melted butter
1/4 teaspoon	1/2 teaspoon	Salt
1/8 teaspoon	1/4 teaspoon	Pepper
1 can (10 1/2-ounce)	2 cans	White clam sauce

Dredge fillets lightly with flour. Arrange in a broiling pan. Combine melted butter, salt, and pepper; drizzle over fillets. Broil for 5 minutes; spoon clam sauce over all and broil 5 minutes more, or until fish flakes easily. Serve at once.

BAKED FISH PIQUANT

To serve 2 or 3:	To serve 4 to 6:	
AMOUNT	AMOUNT	INGREDIENTS
1/2 cup	1 cup	White dinner wine
1 teaspoon	2 teaspoons	Salt
1 pound	2 pounds	Fish fillets (sole, halibut, etc.)
1/4 cup	1/2 cup	Fine dry bread crumbs
1/2 cup	1 cup	Mayonnaise
1/2 cup	1 cup	Dairy sour cream
1/4 cup	1/2 cup	Chopped onions
Several dashes	Several dashes	Paprika

Mix wine and salt; marinate fish fillets in this mixture for 1 hour, turning frequently. Drain fillets thoroughly on paper towels. Dip both sides of fillets in crumbs; arrange side by side in a greased shallow baking dish. Mix mayonnaise and sour cream; add onions and spread evenly over fish. Cover with a thin layer of crumbs; dust with paprika. Bake in a very hot (500°F.) oven for 10 minutes, or until fish flakes when tested with a fork. Serve lemon wedges with it, if desired.

BROILED FISH

To serve 2 or 3:	To serve 4 to 6:	
AMOUNT	AMOUNT	INGREDIENTS
3/4 pound	1 1/2 pounds	Fish fillets (flounder, haddock, etc.)
1 tablespoon	2 tablespoons	Butter
1/4 teaspoon	1/2 teaspoon	Salt
1/8 teaspoon	1/4 teaspoon	Pepper
2 tablespoons	4 tablespoons	Lemon juice

Arrange fillets on a broiling pan. Dot with tiny pieces of butter. Sprinkle with salt, pepper, and lemon juice. Broil 10 minutes, or until fish flakes easily. Serve with tartar sauce or with wedges of lemon.

FISH ROLLS WITH SHRIMP FILLING

To serve 2 to 4:

AMOUNT	INGREDIENTS
4 fillets	Sole or haddock
1 package (3 1/2-ounce)	Danish cheese-and-shrimp spread
1	Egg, beaten
1/2 cup	Fine bread crumbs
4 tablespoons	Butter
1 medium	Onion, coarsely chopped
1/2 pint	Cream
1/3 cup	Tomato sauce
1/4 teaspoon	Salt
1/8 teaspoon	Pepper
1/4 teaspoon	Curry powder

Spread fillets with shrimp cheese spread and roll each fillet. Dip in beaten egg and bread crumbs. Melt butter in a skillet; sauté onion until translucent, then push aside. Fry fish rolls until they turn light brown. Combine cream, tomato sauce, salt, pepper, and curry; pour over fish and simmer for a few minutes. Serve at once.

POACHED SALMON WITH DILL-CUCUMBER SAUCE

To serve 2:	To serve 4:	
AMOUNT (SALMON)	AMOUNT (SALMON)	INGREDIENTS
2 slices	4 slices	Salmon steak, 1 inch thick
1 tablespoon	2 tablespoons	Lemon juice
1/2 teaspoon	1 teaspoon	Salt
1/8 teaspoon	1/4 teaspoon	Pepper
AMOUNT (SAUCE)	AMOUNT (SAUCE)	
2 tablespoons	1/4 cup	Mayonnaise
2 tablespoons	1/4 cup	Dairy sour cream
1/4 cup	1/2 cup	Chopped cucumber
1 teaspoon	2 teaspoons	Dill

Arrange salmon slices in a skillet; pour boiling water to cover fish. Add lemon juice, salt, and pepper. Simmer for 10 minutes, until fish is tender. Remove with a slotted spatula to a platter. Stir mayonnaise and sour cream together; add chopped cucumber and dill; serve with salmon slices.

BROILED LOBSTER TAILS

For each serving:

AMOUNT	INGREDIENTS
1 large or 2 small	Lobster tails
1 teaspoon	Melted butter
1/8 teaspoon	Salt
Dash	Pepper
SAUCE:	
2 tablespoons	Melted butter
1 tablespoon	Lemon juice

With a kitchen scissors or sharp knife, slit membrane and fold back or remove. Arrange tails with hard shells up and broil for 5 minutes; turn so that lobster meat is exposed and paint with melted butter. Season with salt and pepper and broil for an additional 4 to 5 minutes, being careful to avoid overcooking as meat will toughen. Serve at once with a sauce of melted butter and lemon juice served in a small dish on the side of the lobster.

Confucius say that all dishes should have five flavors—sweet, sour, peppery, bitter, and salty. Here is a version of shrimp suey that meets with Oriental tastes. Follow it with sliced pineapple to refresh your palate.

SHRIMP SUEY

To serve 2 or 3:	To serve 4 to 6:	
AMOUNT	AMOUNT	INGREDIENTS
1 package (8-ounce)	2 packages	Frozen shrimp, peeled and deveined
1/4 cup	1/2 cup	Butter
2	4	Sliced onions
1 cup	2 cups	Sliced celery
1	2	Green peppers, seeded and sliced
1 can (20-ounces)	2 cans	Bean sprouts
1 1/2 tablespoons	3 tablespoons	Cornstarch
3/4 cup	1 1/2 cups	Cold water
2 tablespoons	1/4 cup	Soy sauce
1 cup	2 cups	Cooked rice
1/4 teaspoon	1/2 teaspoon	Salt
1/8 teaspoon	1/4 teaspoon	Pepper

Clean shrimp if necessary, but do not cook. Melt butter in skillet and sauté onion, celery, and green pepper until soft. Drain bean sprouts and add liquid to sautéed vegetables. Dissolve cornstarch in the cold water and add to mixture; Add soy sauce and stir over low heat until mixture thickens. Season with salt and pepper. Add drained bean sprouts and raw shrimp, let come to a boil, and cook until shrimp are pink, about 5 minutes. Serve immediately with hot rice.

CURRIED SHRIMP FOR ONE

To make 1 serving:

AMOUNT	INGREDIENTS
1 can (8-ounce)	Stewed tomatoes
1 can (4 1/2-ounce)	Deveined medium shrimp
1/2 teaspoon	Curry powder
1 teaspoon	Cornstarch
1/2 cup	Cooked rice

Combine stewed tomatoes and shrimp in a saucepan. Combine curry powder and cornstarch in a cup; spoon in some juice from the tomatoes until you can stir it to a smooth, thin paste, then return this mixture to the tomato mixture. Heat and stir constantly until mixture is thickened and heated through. Serve over hot rice.

SEAFOOD SUPREME

To serve 2 or 3:	*To serve 4 to 6:*	
AMOUNT	AMOUNT	INGREDIENTS
1/3 cup	2/3 cup	Finely diced onion
1 tablespoon	2 tablespoons	Vegetable oil
1 package (12-ounce)	2 packages	Frozen scallops
1 package (7-ounce)	2 packages	Frozen shrimp
1 can (8-ounce)	2 cans	Tomato sauce with mushrooms
2 tablespoons	1/4 cup	Chopped parsley
2 tablespoons	1/4 cup	Cornstarch
1 teaspoon	2 teaspoons	Worcestershire sauce
1/2 teaspoon	1 teaspoon	Salt
1/3 cup	2/3 cup	Evaporated milk
1/4 cup	1/2 cup	Dry white wine
2 cups	4 cups	Hot cooked rice

Cook scallops and shrimp as directed on the packages. Lightly brown onion in oil; add cooked scallops and shrimp and cook for several minutes. Add tomato sauce, parsley, cornstarch, Worcestershire sauce, and salt. Simmer and stir for 5 minutes. Stir in milk and wine. Heat through over low heat. Serve over hot rice.

SHRIMP RIVIERA

To serve 2 or 3:	*To serve 4 to 6:*	
AMOUNT	AMOUNT	INGREDIENTS
1 pound	2 pounds	Raw shrimp
1 1/2 tablespoons	3 tablespoons	Butter
3/4 cup	1 1/2 cups	Chopped celery
1 small	1 medium	Sliced onion
1 small clove	1 large clove	Garlic, minced
1 1/2 teaspoons	1 tablespoon	Flour
1 cup	2 cups	Canned tomatoes
1/2 cup	1 cup (8-ounce can)	Canned tomato sauce
1 tablespoon	2 tablespoons	Chopped parsley
1/2 teaspoon	1 teaspoon	Oregano
1/2 teaspoon	1 teaspoon	Salt
Dash	Dash or two	Pepper
1/4 cup	1/2 cup	Pitted black olives

Peel and devein shrimp (unless using frozen cleaned shrimp). Melt butter in a large skillet. Add celery, onion, and garlic; cook until vegetables are tender. Sprinkle in flour and stir until lightly browned. Add tomatoes, tomato sauce, parsley, and oregano; season to taste with salt and pepper. Simmer 10 minutes. Add shrimp and olives; simmer 3 minutes, or until shrimp are pink. Serve on hot fluffy rice, if desired.

SHRIMP ROMANO

To serve 6:	*To serve 12:*	
AMOUNT	AMOUNT	INGREDIENTS
2 pounds	4 pounds	Raw shrimp
1/3 cup	2/3 cup	Butter
1/2 cup	1 cup	Sliced green onions
1 cup	2 cups	White wine
1 cup	2 cups	Canned tomatoes
1/3 cup	2/3 cup	Chopped parsley
4 cups	8 cups	Hot cooked rice

Wash, shell, and devein shrimp (this will take you 15 to 20 minutes per pound so leave enough time to do it). In a large skillet, sauté onions in butter until onions are transparent. Add wine, tomatoes, and chopped parsley. Simmer for 30 minutes. Add shrimp and simmer until shrimp turns pink, about 5 minutes. Serve about 1½ cups of shrimp mixture on a bed of ¾ cup rice for each serving. This recipe may be prepared in advance, adding shrimp just before serving time, if desired.

Everyone loves Paella—a Spanish seafood mixture that has a bit of saffron for flavor and color. Here is an easy recipe that will serve a small party.

PAELLA

To serve 6:

AMOUNT	INGREDIENTS
1 pound	Fresh or frozen shrimp
1 can (5-ounce)	Lobster
6 to 8	Clams, fresh or canned
1/2 teaspoon	Saffron
1/4 cup	Hot water
2 tablespoons	Salad oil
1/2 cup	Chopped onions
1/4 cup	Chopped celery
1 clove	Garlic, minced
1 1/2 cups	Uncooked rice
3 cups	Chicken broth (may be canned)
2 teaspoons	Salt
1/2 teaspoon	Oregano
1/4 teaspoon	Pepper
2	Pimientos, chopped
2 cups	Cooked peas

Clean shrimp if necessary. Cook by simmering 1 to 3 minutes. Drain lobster and separate pieces, removing any small bones. If clams are fresh, scrub them well and place them in a covered kettle with about 1 inch of water. Soften saffron in hot water. Heat salad oil in a large saucepan. Add onion, celery, and garlic and cook over low heat until onion is tender. Add rice and cook, stirring, until lightly browned. Add chicken broth (canned or made with 3 chicken bouillon cubes and 3 cups hot water) and salt. Add saffron water, poured through a strainer to remove saffron bits. Bring liquid to a boil. Cover and cook over low heat about 15 minutes, or until liquid is absorbed. While rice is cooking, steam clams about 10 minutes, or until they open. Stir oregano, pepper, pimiento, and peas into rice. Arrange rice, shrimp, lobster, and clams in a buttered ovenproof casserole. Cover and heat 10 minutes at 350°F. Serve at once.

For a change of pace, serve Salmonburgers. Pop them on a hamburger bun with tartar sauce, or on a plate with vegetables and rice. Either way they're a deliciously different change from the daily routine.

SALMONBURGERS

To serve 2 or 4:	To serve 4 to 8:	
AMOUNT	AMOUNT	INGREDIENTS
1 can (8-ounce)	1 can (1 pound)	Red salmon
9	18	Saltine crackers, crushed fine
3/4 tablespoon	1 1/2 tablespoons	Instant minced onion (or fresh)
1	1	Egg
1/4 cup	2/3 cup	Evaporated milk
1 tablespoon	2 tablespoons	Lemon juice
2 tablespoons	3 tablespoons	Butter
4	8	Sandwich buns, split, toasted and buttered (optional)

Remove skin and bones from salmon and discard. With a fork, flake salmon in its liquid in a mixing bowl. Add cracker crumbs, instant minced onion, egg, evaporated milk, and lemon juice. Mix well, then let stand about 5 minutes to allow crumbs to soak up some of the moisture. Melt butter in a large skillet or griddle. Measure ⅓ cup portions of salmon mixture and turn mounds into skillet, leaving space between the mounds. Cook over low heat, flattening salmon slightly as it cooks to form patties the size of the sandwich buns. Cook until golden brown, about 5 minutes; turn patties and cook to brown second side, about 5 minutes longer. Serve with tartar sauce, if desired.

You can rely on tuna to bail you out of a budget dilemma. Here are some mouth-watering ways to take advantage of tuna's high-protein, low-cost opportunities.

TUNA NOODLE CASSEROLE

To serve 2 or 3:	*To serve 4 to 6:*	
AMOUNT	AMOUNT	INGREDIENTS
1 package (10-ounce)	2 packages	5-minute-cook frozen mixed vegetables
1 can (10 1/2-ounce)	2 cans	Condensed cream of mushroom soup
3/4 cup	1 1/2 cups	Milk
1 can (7-ounce)	2 cans	Tuna, drained and flaked
1/2 cup	1 cup	Grated Cheddar cheese
4 ounces	8 ounces	Egg noodles, cooked and drained
2 tablespoons	1/4 cup	Finely chopped onions (or instant minced)
1/2 teaspoon	1 teaspoon	Prepared mustard
1/4 teaspoon	1/2 teaspoon	Salt
1 1/2 cups	3 cups	Grape-nuts flakes
1 tablespoon	2 tablespoons	Melted butter

Place vegetables in saucepan with soup and milk. Bring to a boil over low heat, separating vegetables with a fork to hasten thawing. Remove from heat. Add tuna, cheese, noodles, onion, mustard, and salt. Mix lightly. Pour into a shallow baking dish. Bake at 400°F. for about 15 minutes, or until mixture begins to bubble. Combine cereal and melted butter; sprinkle over top of casserole. Continue baking for about 5 minutes longer, or until cereal is browned. Serve hot.

CHEESE AND TUNA CASSEROLE

To serve 2 or 3:	To serve 4 to 6:	
AMOUNT	AMOUNT	INGREDIENTS
1 tablespoon	2 tablespoons	Butter
1 tablespoon	2 tablespoons	Flour
1/2 cup	1 cup	Milk
1/8 teaspoon	1/4 teaspoon	Salt
1/8 teaspoon	1/4 teaspoon	Onion salt
1/4 teaspoon	1/2 teaspoon	Monosodium glutamate (optional)
1 can (7-ounce)	2 cans	Tuna
1/2 cup	1 cup	Crushed potato chips
1/2 cup	1 cup	Grated American cheese

Melt butter in a saucepan, stir in flour; gradually stir in milk. Stir constantly until sauce thickens to a boiling point; add salt, onion salt, and monosodium glutamate. Combine sauce with tuna and pour into a casserole. Top with crushed potato chips and grated cheese. Bake in a 350°F. oven for 20 minutes. Serve at once.

TUNABURGERS

To serve 2 or 3:	To serve 4 to 6:	
AMOUNT	AMOUNT	INGREDIENTS
1	2	Eggs
2 cups	4 cups	Fine soft bread crumbs
1/4 cup	1/2 cup	Mayonnaise
2 teaspoons	4 teaspoons	Prepared mustard
1 teaspoon	2 teaspoons	Lemon juice
1/2 teaspoon	1 teaspoon	Salt
1/4 cup	1/2 cup	Minced green pepper
2 tablespoons	1/4 cup	Minced fresh onions (or instant minced)
1 can (7-ounce)	2 cans	Tuna, drained
1/2 cup	1 cup	Chopped walnuts

Beat egg. Add bread crumbs, mayonnaise, mustard, lemon juice, salt, green pepper, and onion; mix well. Stir in drained and flaked tuna and walnuts. Shape into patties. Brown lightly on both sides in a skillet over medium heat, using a small amount of oil. If desired, top with:

TARTAR SAUCE: Combine ⅓ cup mayonnaise, 2 tablespoons drained sweet pickle relish, 1 teaspoon lemon juice, and a dash of onion salt.

TUNA ZITI MARINARA

To serve 2 or 3:	To serve 4 to 6:	
AMOUNT	AMOUNT	INGREDIENTS
1 can (7-ounce)	2 cans	Tuna, in oil
1 cup	2 cups	Ziti macaroni
2 tablespoons	1/4 cup	Olive oil
2 tablespoons	3 tablespoons	Butter
1 clove	1 clove	Garlic, halved
3 tablespoons	1 can (6-ounce)	Tomato paste
1/4 cup	1/2 cup	Water
1/2 can	1 can (15-ounce)	Tomato sauce with tomato pieces
1/2 teaspoon	1 teaspoon	Salt
1/8 teaspoon	1/4 teaspoon	Pepper
3/4 teaspoon	1 1/2 teaspoons	Sugar
1/4 cup	1/2 cup	Grated Parmesan cheese

Drain oil from tuna into boiling salted water, following direction amounts on package of ziti; add ziti and cook as directed on package.

While ziti is cooking, prepare marinara sauce. Heat olive oil and butter in a large skillet; add garlic for several minutes, then discard garlic. Add tomato paste and cook, stirring constantly, over medium heat for about 5 minutes. Stir in water, tomato sauce, salt, pepper, and sugar. Bring to a boil; add tuna. Cook, stirring until tuna is heated, about 10 minutes. On a serving platter, sprinkle half the cheese over drained ziti, and add a little sauce; mix well. Top with remaining sauce and cheese.

HOT TUNA CASSEROLE

To serve 2 or 3:	To serve 4 to 6:	
AMOUNT	AMOUNT	INGREDIENTS
1 can (10 1/2-ounce)	2 cans	Condensed cream of mushroom soup
1/2 teaspoon	1 teaspoon	Oregano
1/2 teaspoon	1 teaspoon	Salt
1 tablespoon	2 tablespoons	Minced fresh onions (or instant minced)
1 can (1-pound)	2 cans	Cut green beans
2 cans (7-ounces each)	4 cans	Tuna
1 cup	2 cups	Packaged pre-cooked rice
1 tablespoon	1 tablespoon	Grated Parmesan cheese

Put undiluted cream of mushroom soup, oregano, salt, and minced onions in a saucepan. Drain liquid from beans into a measuring cup; add enough water to make 1¼ cups for the 2-to-3 amount, and 2½ cups for the 4-to-6 amount. Stir liquid into soup mixture; add tuna. Bring to a boil, stirring occasionally. Stir in rice; remove from heat. Turn into a casserole; arrange beans around the edge and sprinkle with Parmesan cheese. Cover. Bake in a 400°F. oven for 20 minutes. Serve at once.

BLUE CHEESE–TUNA CASSEROLE

To serve 2 or 3:	To serve 4 to 6:	
AMOUNT	AMOUNT	INGREDIENTS
1 1/2 cups	3 cups	Cooked rice
1 tablespoon	2 tablespoons	Butter
1 tablespoon	2 tablespoons	Flour
1 cup	2 cups	Milk
1/4 cup	1/2 cup	Crumbled blue cheese
8 slices	12 slices	Tomato
1 can (7-ounce)	2 cans	Tuna

Cook rice according to package directions. In a saucepan melt butter; stir in flour. Remove from heat; gradually stir in milk. Cook, stirring constantly, until slightly thickened. Cook 2 additional minutes. Add blue cheese and stir until cheese is melted. Place rice in casserole; top with half the slices of tomato, then tuna. Pour cheese sauce over all; bake 20 minutes. Remove from oven; garnish with remaining tomato slices. Return to oven 10 to 15 minutes more. Serve hot.

12 · Winning Vegetables

Colorful and well-prepared vegetables are the accents of attractive cuisine. You can use them to give a platter a touch of green, red, or yellow to please the eye before you please the palate.

If you already have a variety of vegetables you are able to prepare simply but effectively, you will savor the collection in this chapter as it will introduce you to new ways of serving these holders of valuable vitamins and minerals. Get in the habit of slipping a seasoned tomato half under the broiler with your meat, or baking a vegetable casserole with your roast. If you can rid yourself of childhood-based taste preferences, you will find a broad variety of new and colorful dishes to try, and hopefully to enjoy.

There are only a few important rules to remember about vegetable cookery. Wash all fresh produce carefully before cooking and, to preserve their nutrients, cook in the least amount of liquid possible. When peeling vegetables, try to keep your cuttings thin so you don't throw away valuable minerals. Avoid reheating vegetables as they lose flavor and vitamins, making it almost worthless to re-serve them at all.

An easy way to remember whether or not to cover the pot: If it grows under the ground, cover it; if it grows above ground, don't!

In order to keep the freshest colors, the French "blanch" (dip in boiling water for a moment and then into iced water to stop the cooking action) their green vegetables, and then proceed to cook them just before serving. Another method of preserving color is to add lemon juice; this prevents white vegetables from turning light tan, red vegetables from turning brown. Yellow vegetables such as carrots and sweet potatoes do not need any additives to preserve their color, and are cooked covered.

Cook frozen vegetables as directed on the package, using as little water as possible. A good technique for heating canned vegetables is to drain off the liquid into a saucepan and heat the liquid until it reduces to half the amount, then add the vegetables and heat in this double-strength juice. Since canned vegetables are already cooked, only a few moments are required to bring them to serving temperature.

Always keep color and variety in mind, both for eye appeal and balanced nutrition, as you plan to use nature's valuable accessories to enhance your meals.

ASPARAGUS WITH PECAN SAUCE

To serve 2 or 3:	To serve 4 to 6:	
AMOUNT	AMOUNT	INGREDIENTS
3/4 pound	1 1/2 pounds	Asparagus
2 tablespoons	4 tablespoons	Butter
1/4 teaspoon	1/2 teaspoon	Onion powder
1/2 teaspoon	1 teaspoon	Lemon juice
1/8 teaspoon	1/4 teaspoon	Salt
1/4 cup	1/2 cup	Coarsely chopped pecans

Cook asparagus in a small amount of water. Meanwhile, in a small skillet melt butter; stir in onion powder, lemon juice, and salt. Add pecans and sauté 5 minutes. Drain asparagus and place on a platter; pour pecan sauce over asparagus. Serve at once.

BEAN-AND-TOMATO STEW

To serve 2 or 3:	*To serve 4 to 6:*	
AMOUNT	AMOUNT	INGREDIENTS
1 can (8-ounce)	1 can (1-pound)	Stewed tomatoes
1 can (8-ounce)	1 can (1-pound)	French-cut green beans
1 1/2 teaspoons	1 tablespoon	Cornstarch
2 tablespoons	1/4 cup	Water
1 teaspoon	2 teaspoons	Butter
2 strips	4 strips	Cooked, crumbled bacon

Combine stewed tomatoes and green beans in a saucepan. Stir cornstarch into water until smooth, then add it to the vegetables in the saucepan. Heat and stir until thickened and smooth. Add butter and heat until melted. Add crumbled bacon. Serve hot.

GREEN BEANS WITH CHEESE

To serve 2 or 3:	*To serve 4 to 6:*	
AMOUNT	AMOUNT	INGREDIENTS
1 package (10-ounce)	2 packages	Frozen green beans
1/4 cup	1/2 cup	Danish mushroom-cheese spread

Cook frozen beans according to package directions; drain, and return to saucepan. Add cheese and toss lightly so the heat of the beans melts the cheese. Serve at once.

SWEET-AND-SOUR BEETS

To serve 2 or 3:	To serve 4 to 6:	
AMOUNT	AMOUNT	INGREDIENTS
1 tablespoon	2 tablespoons	Butter
1 1/2 teaspoons	1 tablespoon	Cornstarch
1/2 cup	1 cup	Drained beet juice
1 1/2 teaspoons	1 tablespoon	Sugar
1 teaspoon	2 teaspoons	Dried minced onions
1 tablespoon	2 tablespoons	Wine vinegar
1/4 teaspoon	1/2 teaspoon	Salt
Dash	1/8 teaspoon	Pepper
1 can (1-pound)	2 cans	Sliced beets, drained

Melt butter in a saucepan; stir in cornstarch, beet juice, sugar, onion, vinegar, salt, and pepper. Stir until sauce thickens; cook about 2 minutes more, stirring constantly. Add beets and let stand on range for 10 minutes. Heat a moment just before serving.

BROCCOLI WITH POLONAISE SAUCE

To serve 2 or 3:	To serve 4 to 6:	
AMOUNT	AMOUNT	INGREDIENTS
1 package (10-ounce)	2 packages	Frozen broccoli spears
1/4 cup	1/2 cup	Butter
1/4 teaspoon	1/2 teaspoon	Salt
1/2 cup	1 cup	Chopped mushrooms
2 tablespoons	4 tablespoons	Lemon juice
1/4 cup	1/2 cup	Bread crumbs
1	2	Hard-cooked eggs, sieved

Cook broccoli as directed on the package. Meanwhile, in a skillet melt butter; stir in salt. Toss mushrooms with lemon juice; add to skillet and sauté a few minutes. Stir in bread crumbs. Drain broccoli and arrange on a platter; top with mushroom-bread crumb mixture and sprinkle sieved egg over all. Serve at once.

GLAZED CARROTS

To serve 3 to 4:	*To serve 6 to 8:*	
AMOUNT	AMOUNT	INGREDIENTS
1 can (1-pound)	2 cans	Sliced carrots
1 tablespoon	2 tablespoons	Butter
1/4 cup	1/2 cup	Carrot liquid
1/3 cup	2/3 cup	Light brown sugar
Dash	Dash or two	Salt

Heat canned carrots in own liquid, reserving the amount of carrot liquid needed in the list of ingredients. In a separate saucepan, combine butter, carrot liquid, brown sugar, and salt. Bring to a boil; simmer 2 minutes. Drain carrots and place in serving dish. Pour glaze over carrots and mix to coat thoroughly. Serve at once.

CORN WITH ONION-PARSLEY SAUCE

To serve 2 or 3:	*To serve 4 to 6:*	
AMOUNT	AMOUNT	INGREDIENTS
1 can (16-ounce)	2 cans	Corn niblets
2 tablespoons	4 tablespoons	Butter
1 tablespoon	2 tablespoons	Chopped parsley
1 1/2 teaspoons	1 tablespoon	Grated onion
1 teaspoon	2 teaspoons	Worcestershire sauce
1/4 teaspoon	1/2 teaspoon	Salt
1/8 teaspoon	1/4 teaspoon	Pepper
1/8 teaspoon	1/4 teaspoon	Dry mustard

Empty corn into a saucepan. Meanwhile, in a small mixing bowl cream the butter until soft; gradually add parsley, onion, and Worcestershire sauce. Blend in salt, pepper, and dry mustard. Then blend this mixture thoroughly through the corn in the saucepan. Simmer over low heat, stirring occasionally, until hot for serving.

CHEESE-CORN MEXICALI

To serve 2 or 3:	To serve 4 to 6:	
AMOUNT	AMOUNT	INGREDIENTS
1 tablespoon	2 tablespoons	Butter
2 tablespoons	1/4 cup	Chopped onions
1/2 can	1 can (16-ounces)	Whole kernel corn, drained
1/4 cup	1/2 cup	Sliced, pitted ripe olives
1 tablespoon	2 tablespoons	Flour
1/2 teaspoon	1 teaspoon	Salt
1/8 teaspoon	1/4 teaspoon	Chili powder
Dash	1/8 teaspoon	Pepper
1/2 cup	1 cup	Shredded Cheddar cheese
1/2 can	1 can (8-ounce)	Tomato sauce

In a small skillet, melt butter; sauté onion until tender. In a bowl combine corn, olives, flour, salt, chili powder, pepper, and sautéed onion. Turn into a buttered casserole; sprinkle cheese on top. Pour tomato sauce over all. Bake in a preheated 350° F. oven for 25 to 30 minutes.

LIMA-CORN BAKE

To serve 2 or 3:	To serve 4 to 6:	
AMOUNT	AMOUNT	INGREDIENTS
2 tablespoons	1/4 cup	Butter
1 tablespoon	2 tablespoons	Sliced green onions
1 small	1 large	Garlic clove, split
1/4 teaspoon	1/2 teaspoon	Salt
1/2 package	1 package (10-ounce)	Frozen lima beans
1/2 package	1 package (10-ounce)	Frozen corn niblets
1	2	Tomatoes, sliced
3 tablespoons	6 tablespoons	Fine dry bread crumbs

In a small saucepan melt butter; sauté onion and garlic until onion is tender (about 5 minutes). Remove garlic; add salt. Break frozen vegetables apart. Place lima beans in a shallow casserole; add a layer of tomato slices, then layer all of the corn. Top with remaining tomato slices. Pour ½ of the butter mixture over the vegetables. Cover tightly with foil; bake in a preheated 350° F. oven for 40 minutes. Toss bread crumbs with remaining butter and sprinkle over vegetables. Return to oven and bake, uncovered, for an additional 10 minutes.

This French vegetable dish is fast gaining popularity with those who love eggplant and zucchini. It is best served hot, but even as a cold leftover it has palate appeal.

RATATOUILLE

To serve 2 or 3:	*To serve 4 to 6:*	
AMOUNT	AMOUNT	INGREDIENTS
2 tablespoons	4 tablespoons	Butter
1/2 cup	1 cup	Thinly sliced onions
1 small	1 large	Garlic clove, finely chopped
1	2	Zucchini, cut in 1/2-inch slices
1 small	1 medium	Eggplant, peeled and cut into cubes
1/4 cup	1/2 cup	Flour
1	2	Green peppers, cut into strips
1	2	Tomatoes, cut in wedges
1/2 teaspoon	1 teaspoon	Salt
1/8 teaspoon	1/4 teaspoon	Oregano
Dash	1/8 teaspoon	Pepper

Melt butter in large skillet. Sauté onions and garlic until onions are tender. Dip zucchini and eggplant in flour to coat lightly. Add to onions along with green pepper; cover and simmer for 30 minutes. Add tomatoes, salt, oregano, and pepper. Cook an additional 15 minutes.

ONIONS WITH CRUNCHY CREAM SAUCE

To serve 4:

AMOUNT	INGREDIENTS
1 can (1 pound)	Whole onions, heated and drained
1 can (10 1/2-ounce)	Condensed cream of mushroom soup
3 tablespoons	Light cream
1/3 cup	Grape-nuts cereal
1/2 cup	Grated Cheddar cheese

Place onions in lightly greased shallow 1-quart baking dish. Combine soup, cream, and cereal. Pour over onions. Sprinkle with cheese. Broil about 5 or 10 minutes, or until cheese melts and browns. Serve at once.

MINTED PEAS

To serve 2 or 3:	*To serve 4 to 6:*	
AMOUNT	AMOUNT	INGREDIENTS
1 package (10-ounce)	2 packages	Frozen peas
2 tablespoons	4 tablespoons	Butter
3/4 teaspoon	1 1/2 teaspoons	Dried mint
1/4 teaspoon	1/2 teaspoon	Sugar
1/4 teaspoon	1/2 teaspoon	Salt

In a casserole, melt butter in the oven. Add mint, sugar, and salt. Break up peas; mix with butter. Cover and bake in a 350° F. oven for 40 minutes.

BAKED SPINACH GOURMET

To serve 4 or 6:

AMOUNT	INGREDIENTS
2 packages (10-ounce)	Frozen chopped spinach
1 can (10 1/2-ounce)	Condensed cream of mushroom soup
1 can (3 1/2-ounce)	French fried onions
2 tablespoons	Grated Parmesan cheese

Cook frozen spinach according to package directions; drain thoroughly. Empty into a flat baking dish; add condensed cream of mushroom soup and ½ of the fried onions. Stir thoroughly; top with remaining onions and sprinkle cheese over the top. Bake in a 350° F. oven for 20 minutes. Serve hot.

BAKED STUFFED TOMATOES

To serve 2 or 3:	To serve 4 to 6:	
AMOUNT	AMOUNT	INGREDIENTS
2 or 3	4 to 6	Medium tomatoes
1 cup	2 cups	Seasoned croutons
1 can (4 1/2-ounce)	2 cans	Deviled ham

Remove tops from tomatoes; scoop out pulp. Combine croutons and deviled ham and fill tomatoes. Place in a shallow baking dish; barely cover the bottom of dish with hot water and bake at 375° F. for about 15 minutes. Serve at once.

ZUCCHINI WITH MUSHROOM SAUCE

To serve 2 or 3:	To serve 4 to 6:	
AMOUNT	AMOUNT	INGREDIENTS
2	4	Medium zucchini
2 tablespoons	4 tablespoons	Butter
2 teaspoons	4 teaspoons	Lemon juice
1/2 cup	1 cup	Sliced mushrooms
1/4 teaspoon	1/2 teaspoon	Salt
1/8 teaspoon	1/4 teaspoon	Thyme
Dash	Dash or two	Pepper

Wash zucchini; cut into diagonal slices. Place in small amount of water in a deep saucepan. Cover and bring to a steam; reduce heat and simmer about 10 minutes. Drain if water has not been completely absorbed. Meanwhile, in a small skillet, melt butter; toss mushrooms with lemon juice and add to skillet. Add salt, thyme, and pepper; sauté for 5 minutes. Pour over hot zucchini and serve.

SWEET POTATO CASSEROLE

To serve 4 to 6:

AMOUNT	INGREDIENTS
1 can (23-ounce)	**Small whole sweet potatoes in syrup**
2 tablespoons	**Butter**
1/2 teaspoon	**Salt**
1/4 teaspoon	**Nutmeg**
1	**Egg, beaten**
1 can (8 3/4-ounce)	**Pineapple tidbits, drained**
1 tablespoon	**Brown sugar**

Empty sweet potatoes into a casserole; mash with butter, salt, and nutmeg. Stir in egg. Stir in pineapple tidbits. Sprinkle brown sugar over top. Bake at 350° F. for 20 minutes.

BAKED POTATO

For each serving:

AMOUNT	INGREDIENTS
1	**Baking potato**
1	**Pat butter**
1/8 teaspoon	**Salt**
1 tablespoon	**Dairy sour cream (optional)**
1 teaspoon	**Chopped chives (optional)**

Wash potato well. Wrap in aluminum foil for faster cooking, if desired. Bake in 350° F. oven for 55 to 60 minutes; prick with a fork to test tenderness, and if necessary, bake a while longer. When fork pierces easily, remove from oven, cut a cross in the top of the potato, and press sides together to widen opening. Season with butter and salt. Stir sour cream and chives together and top potato with it. Serve at once.

PARMESAN BAKED POTATO PUFFS

To serve 2:	To serve 4:	
AMOUNT	AMOUNT	INGREDIENTS
1 large	2 large	Baking potatoes
3 tablespoons	1/3 cup	Milk
1 tablespoon	2 tablespoons	Butter
1/4 teaspoon	1/2 teaspoon	Salt
Dash	Dash	Pepper
2 teaspoons	4 teaspoons	Grated Parmesan cheese

Wash potatoes and bake in a preheated 350° F. oven for 1 hour, or until fork-tender. Cut potatoes in half lengthwise; scoop out insides with a spoon into a mixing bowl. Mash potatoes; add milk, butter, salt, pepper, and cheese. Beat until fluffy. Spoon mixture back into potato shells, mounding high. Sprinkle tops with Parmesan cheese. Place on baking sheet and return to oven 20 or 30 minutes, or until top is lightly browned. Serve immediately. (These may be prepared earlier and refrigerated until 30 minutes before dinner, when you proceed with the second baking.)

BOILED POTATOES WITH DILL

To serve 2 or 3:	To serve 4 to 6:	
AMOUNT	AMOUNT	INGREDIENTS
3	6	Large potatoes, quartered and peeled
Enough to cover	Enough to cover	Water
1/4 teaspoon	1/2 teaspoon	Salt
1/2 teaspoon	1 teaspoon	Dried dill
1 tablespoon	2 tablespoons	Butter

Place quartered potatoes in a saucepan; cover with water. Add salt and dill and simmer until fork-tender, about 20 minutes. Drain and add butter, tossing lightly until pieces of potato are well coated with butter. Serve at once. Chill leftover potatoes and use for cold potato salad.

BUTTER-FRIED POTATOES

To serve 2 or 3:	*To serve 4 to 6:*	
AMOUNT	AMOUNT	INGREDIENTS
2 tablespoons	1/4 cup	Butter
2 cups	4 cups	Thinly sliced potatoes
1/4 cup	1/2 cup	Chopped onions
2 tablespoons	1/4 cup	Chopped parsley
1/2 teaspoon	1 teaspoon	Salt
Dash	1/8 teaspoon	Pepper

In a large skillet (with cover) melt butter. Add potatoes to skillet; cover and cook over medium heat, turning occasionally for 25 to 30 minutes. Remove cover; add more butter to skillet if necessary. Add onion and parsley. Fry potatoes until golden brown. Add salt and pepper. Serve at once.

13 · Hearty Pastas

Pasta is one of the most popular forms of cooking all over the world. Although we automatically think of Italy when we think of pasta, it is thought to have originated in China and spread out from there. Whatever its origin, pasta is available under many different names —from won ton in Oriental soup to kreplach in Jewish chicken soup, and from cannelloni to noodle pudding. From the thinnest string of a noodle to the broadest one for lasagne, it is all pasta and it is all delectable.

Besides its good taste, pasta is a great expander for small amounts of meat and cheese that have to feed a lot of people in an appetizing way. So try some of these recipes when your budget is limping, or when you are entertaining too many for roast beef, or when you are hungry for something different and good.

Experiment until you find the forms you prefer, and cook them according to the recipe or package directions. One good rule of thumb when boiling pasta: Provide at least four quarts of water to every pound of pasta that you are cooking. Add a tablespoon of cooking oil to the salted water and you will eliminate the problem of stickiness when you drain. Cook until *al dente,* just right to the bite, then drain at once. Proceed immediately with the recipe. If you have to hold pasta for a while, mix sauce, butter, or broth through it to keep it from becoming a sticky mass. When making lasagne, immerse the broad noodles in cold water during the preparations as the cooked drained noodles will be difficult to handle otherwise. Slip each strand into a colander to dry for a moment before you add it to the cheese-and-sauce slathered layers.

It's a good idea to have spaghetti, macaroni, and noodles on your pantry shelf as emergency fare. A can of red or white clam sauce, a bit of browned ground meat cooked in tomato sauce with a dash of seasonings, or just butter and Parmesan cheese can turn that pasta into a nice dinner offering.

And do explore the other types of pasta available in your market. You'll be surprised at the variety of shapes that are packaged for your selection.

SPAGHETTI WITH TOMATO-MEAT SAUCE

To serve 2 or 3:	*To serve 4 to 6:*	
AMOUNT	AMOUNT	INGREDIENTS
1 1/2 tablespoons	3 tablespoons	Olive oil
1 small	1 large	Onion, chopped
1 clove	2 cloves	Garlic, mashed
1/2 pound	1 pound	Ground beef
1 tablespoon	2 tablespoons	Dried parsley
1/2 teaspoon	1 teaspoon	Salt
1/4 teaspoon	1/2 teaspoon	Ground black pepper
1/4 teaspoon	1/2 teaspoon	Dried oregano
1 can (6-ounce)	2 cans	Tomato paste
1 can (1-pound)	1 can (2-pound 3-oz.)	Tomatoes packed in sauce (or puree) with basil leaf.
1 teaspoon	2 teaspoons	Sugar

Heat olive oil in the bottom of a saucepan; add onion and garlic and cook until onion is translucent. Add broken up bits of ground beef, separating into tinier particles with a fork while browning. Add parsley, salt, pepper, and oregano, stirring well into the meat mixture. Add tomato paste, tomatoes packed in sauce, and then sugar; stir all together well. Lower heat and cook for 1 to 1½ hours, stirring occasionally. Serve over cooked spaghetti.

This meal-in-one can be prepared in minutes, and most of the ingredients can be kept on the cupboard shelf for just such an emergency. It's tasty, filling, and economical.

SPAGHETTI WITH TUNA-ONION SAUCE

To serve 2:	To serve 4:	
AMOUNT	AMOUNT	INGREDIENTS
1 1/2 teaspoons	1 tablespoon	Salt
1 1/2 quarts	3 quarts	Boiling water
4 ounces	8 ounces	Spaghetti
2 tablespoons	1/4 cup	Butter
2 tablespoons	1/4 cup	Flour
1/2 teaspoon	1 teaspoon	Salt
Dash	1/8 teaspoon	Pepper
Dash	Dash	Nutmeg
1 cup	2 cups	Milk
1 can (7-ounce)	2 cans	Tuna, drained
1/2 can	1 can (16-ounce)	Whole onions, drained
2 tablespoons	1/4 cup	Sliced ripe (black) olives
1/2	1	Pimiento (canned), cut in strips

Add salt to rapidly boiling water. Gradually add spaghetti so that water continues to boil. Cook uncovered, stirring occasionally, until tender. Drain in colander. Melt butter in saucepan; blend in flour, second listing of salt, pepper, and nutmeg. Gradually add milk; cook stirring constantly until sauce boils, about 1 minute. Stir in remaining ingredients. Heat and serve on spaghetti.

SPAGHETTI WITH RED CLAM SAUCE

To serve 2 or 3:	*To serve 4 to 6:*	
AMOUNT	AMOUNT	INGREDIENTS
1/2 pound	1 pound	Spaghetti
1 can (10 1/2-ounce)	2 cans	Red clam sauce
Pinch	2 pinches	Crushed red pepper
Dash	1/8 teaspoon	Black pepper
1 teaspoon	2 teaspoons	Dried parsley

Cook spaghetti as directed on the package; drain. Meanwhile, empty clam sauce into a small saucepan; add red pepper (more if you like it "hot"), black pepper, and dried parsley. Heat while spaghetti is cooking, stirring occasionally. Pour over drained spaghetti and serve at once.

LINGUINI WITH WHITE CLAM SAUCE

To serve 2 or 3:	*To serve 4 to 6:*	
AMOUNT	AMOUNT	INGREDIENTS
1/2 pound	1 pound	Linguini (slender flat spaghetti)
1 can (10 1/2-ounce)	2 cans	White clam sauce
1 clove	2 cloves	Garlic, chopped
1 teaspoon	2 teaspoons	Dried parsley
Pinch	Pinch or two	Crushed red pepper
Dash	1/8 teaspoon	Ground black pepper

Cook linguini as directed on the package; drain. Meanwhile, empty clam sauce into a small saucepan; add chopped garlic, parsley, red pepper, and black pepper. Heat while linguini is cooking, stirring occasionally. Pour over drained linguini and serve at once.

NOODLES WITH SHRIMP MARINARA

To serve 2:	*To serve 4:*	
AMOUNT	AMOUNT	INGREDIENTS
1 1/2 quarts	3 quarts	Boiling water
1 1/2 teaspoons	1 tablespoon	Salt
2 cups (4 ounces)	4 cups (8 ounces)	Egg noodles
1/2 pound	1 pound	Shrimp, shelled and deveined
3 tablespoons	6 tablespoons	Sliced pimiento-stuffed olives
3 tablespoons	6 tablespoons	Chopped pecans (optional)
2 tablespoons	1/4 cup	Chopped onions
1 1/2 teaspoons	1 tablespoon	Olive oil
1 can (8-ounce)	2 cans	Tomato sauce
2 tablespoons	1/4 cup	Water
1/8 teaspoon	1/4 teaspoon	Salt
1/8 teaspoon	1/4 teaspoon	Thyme
Dash	Dash	Pepper

Add salt to rapidly boiling water. Gradually add noodles so that water continues to boil. Cook uncovered, stirring occasionally, until tender. Drain in colander. Meanwhile, in another saucepan, cook shrimp, olives, pecans, and onion in oil until shrimp turns pink, about 2 minutes; stir frequently. Add tomato sauce, water, salt, thyme, and pepper. Cook covered, 10 minutes; remove cover, cook 5 minutes longer. Serve over noodles.

NOODLE BOWS AND CHEESE

To serve 2 or 3:	To serve 4 to 6:	
AMOUNT	AMOUNT	INGREDIENTS
2 tablespoons	1/4 cup	Fine bread crumbs
3/4 tablespoon	1 1/2 tablespoons	Salt
2 quarts	4 quarts	Boiling water
3 cups	6 cups	Egg noodle bows
1 tablespoon	2 tablespoons	Butter
1/2 cup	1 cup	Freshly grated Parmesan cheese
1/2 cup	1 cup	Diced Swiss cheese
1/2 cup	1 cup	Diced mozzarella cheese
1 1/2 tablespoons	3 tablespoons	Butter
1 1/2 tablespoons	3 tablespoons	Flour
1 1/2 cups	3 cups	Milk
3/4 teaspoon	1 1/2 teaspoons	Salt
1/8 teaspoon	1/4 teaspoon	Pepper
Dash	1/8 teaspoon	Nutmeg

Shake bread crumbs into a buttered baking dish to coat the interior. Add salt to rapidly boiling water. Gradually add noodle bows so that water continues to boil. Cook uncovered, stirring occasionally, until tender. Drain in colander. Toss with butter, then Parmesan cheese. Add Swiss and mozzarella cheeses; toss lightly. In a saucepan, melt butter and blend in flour. Gradually add milk; cook, stirring constantly, until sauce boils 1 minute. Add second listing of salt, pepper, and nutmeg. Turn half the noodle mixture into the prepared dish; top with ½ of the white sauce. Repeat layers. Sprinkle extra grated Parmesan cheese or bread crumbs on top, if desired. Bake in a 350° F. oven for 25 minutes. Serve at once.

NOODLES WITH CHILI

To serve 2 or 3:	To serve 4 to 6:	
AMOUNT	AMOUNT	INGREDIENTS
1/2 pound	1 pound	Ground beef
1 1/2 teaspoons	1 tablespoon	Olive oil
1/2 cup	1 cup	Chopped onions
1 small clove	1 large clove	Garlic, minced

To serve 2 or 3:	To serve 4 to 6:	
AMOUNT	AMOUNT	INGREDIENTS
1/2 can	1 can (14-ounce)	Tomatoes
1/2 can	1 can (6-ounce)	Tomato paste
1/4 cup	1/2 cup	Water
1 teaspoon	2 teaspoons	Salt
1 tablespoon	2 tablespoons	Chili powder
1/2 can	1 can (15-ounce)	Kidney beans, drained
1 1/2 teaspoons	1 tablespoon	Salt
1 1/2 quarts	3 quarts	Boiling water
2 cups (4 ounces)	4 cups (8 ounces)	Medium egg noodles

In heavy saucepan, brown beef in olive oil, stirring frequently and breaking apart with a fork. Add onions, garlic, tomatoes, tomato paste, water, salt, and chili powder. Mix well and simmer, covered, for 45 minutes. Add kidney beans and continue cooking for 30 minutes more. About 10 minutes before cooking time is finished, add second listing of salt to rapidly boiling water. Gradually add noodles so that water continues to boil. Cook uncovered, stirring occasionally, until tender. Drain in colander. Serve with chili.

ASPARAGUS-MACARONI CASSEROLE

To serve 3 to 4:	To serve 6 to 8:	
AMOUNT	AMOUNT	INGREDIENTS
1/2 package	1 package (7-ounce)	Elbow macaroni
1/2 pound	1 pound	Fresh asparagus
1/2 can	1 can (10 1/2-ounce)	Condensed cream of mushroom soup
1/2 cup	1 cup	Milk
1 tablespoon	2 tablespoons	Chopped chives
1/4 teaspoon	1/2 teaspoon	Salt
1/8 teaspoon	1/4 teaspoon	Pepper
3/4 cup	1 1/2 cups	Shredded Cheddar cheese
2	4	Hard-cooked eggs, sliced
1/4 cup	1/2 cup	Slivered almonds

Cook macaroni according to package directions; drain. Cook asparagus just until tender; drain and cut into ½-inch pieces, reserving the tops of several spears. In a large bowl gradually add milk to mushroom soup; add chives, salt, pepper. Add ½ cup Cheddar cheese for the 3-to-4 recipe, and 1 cup Cheddar cheese for the 6-to-8 recipe. Add sliced eggs, macaroni, cut asparagus, and almonds. Turn into a buttered casserole. Bake in a preheated 350°F. oven for 40 minutes; then arrange reserved asparagus spears on top; sprinkle on remaining Cheddar cheese. Return to oven about 5 minutes, or until cheese is melted.

The eggs in this dish impart a custardy texture to make this an unusual macaroni-and-cheese offering. Full of protein and inexpensive, it's a great main course when the budget is low.

MACARONI-AND-EGG CASSEROLE

To serve 2 or 3:	To serve 4 to 6:	
AMOUNT	AMOUNT	INGREDIENTS
3/4 teaspoon	1 1/2 teaspoons	Salt
3 cups	6 cups	Boiling water
1/2 cup	1 cup	Elbow macaroni
2 tablespoons	1/4 cup	Butter
1/2 cup	1 cup	Soft bread crumbs
3/4 cup	1 1/2 cups	Milk, scalded
1/2	1	Canned pimiento, minced
1 tablespoon	2 tablespoons	Chopped celery
1 1/2 teaspoons	1 tablespoon	Chopped onions
1/2 teaspoon	1 teaspoon	Salt
Dash	1/8 teaspoon	Pepper
Dash	Dash	Paprika
2	4	Eggs, beaten
3/4 cup	1 1/2 cups	Grated Cheddar cheese

Add salt to rapidly boiling water. Gradually add macaroni so that water continues to boil. Cook uncovered, stirring occasionally, until tender. Drain in colander. Return macaroni to pot, add butter, and toss until butter melts. Add remaining ingredients and mix well. Turn into a greased casserole. Bake in 350° F. oven for 40 minutes. Serve at once.

MACARONI-VEGETABLE CASSEROLE

To serve 2 or 3:	To serve 4 to 6:	
AMOUNT	AMOUNT	INGREDIENTS
1 1/2 quarts	3 quarts	Boiling water
1 1/2 teaspoons	1 tablespoon	Salt
1 cup	2 cups	Uncooked elbow macaroni
1 tablespoon	2 tablespoons	Butter
2 tablespoons	1/4 cup	Minced onions
1 1/2 teaspoons	1 tablespoon	Flour
1/8 teaspoon	1/4 teaspoon	Salt
1/4 teaspoon	1/2 teaspoon	Oregano
Dash	Dash	Pepper
1 cup	2 cups	Milk
1/4 pound	1/2 pound	Grated Cheddar cheese
1/2 can	1 can (17-ounce)	Peas and carrots, drained
1/3 cup	2/3 cup	Italian style bread crumbs
1 1/2 teaspoons	1 tablespoon	Melted butter

Add salt to rapidly boiling water. Gradually add macaroni so that water continues to boil. Cook uncovered, stirring occasionally, until tender. Drain in colander. Melt butter in saucepan; add onion and then quickly stir in flour, salt, oregano, and pepper. Slowly stir in milk; cook, stirring until smooth. Add cheese and stir until melted. Combine sauce with maracroni and peas and carrots in a greased casserole. Top with bread crumbs tossed with melted butter. Bake in 350°F. oven for 20 minutes.

TANGY MACARONI-CHEESE CASSEROLE

To serve 3 or 4:	To serve 6 to 8:	
AMOUNT	AMOUNT	INGREDIENTS
1/2 pound	1 pound	Elbow macaroni
1/2 pound	1 pound	American cheese, grated
1 1/2 cups	3 cups	Milk
1 teaspoon	2 teaspoons	Dry mustard
1/4 teaspoon	1/2 teaspoon	Tabasco sauce

Cook macaroni according to package directions. Drain macaroni and combine with cheese; mix lightly. Place mixture in a buttered casserole. Blend milk with mustard and Tabasco. Pour over macaroni mixture in a greased casserole. Cover. Bake in a 350°F. oven for 35 minutes. Uncover and continue to bake 10 to 15 minutes longer, or until top is lightly browned.

Although this takes a little time to prepare, it is a perfect meal-in-one to serve to casual guests. Present it with a crisp salad and the remaining red dinner wine.

LASAGNE

Serves 6 to 8:

AMOUNT	INGREDIENTS
1 pound	Ground beef
2 tablespoons	Olive oil
1	Large onion, chopped
2 cloves	Garlic, finely chopped
1 teaspoon	Basil
1 teaspoon	Oregano
2 teaspoons	Salt
1 can (1-lb. 14-ounce)	Tomatoes
1 can (6-ounce)	Tomato paste
3/4 cup	Burgundy or claret wine
1/2 pound	Lasagne noodles
1/2 pound	Mozzarella cheese
1/2 cup	Grated Parmesan cheese

Brown beef slowly in oil. Add onion and continue cooking until onion is transparent, stirring frequently. Add garlic, basil, and oregano, and cook a few minutes longer, stirring constantly. Add salt, tomatoes, tomato paste, and wine, and simmer about 1½ hours. Meanwhile, cook lasagne noodles in boiling salted water for 20 minutes; drain and rinse. Slice mozzarella cheese. In a greased flat baking dish, starting and ending with sauce, arrange sauce, noodles, and cheeses in layers. Sprinkle Parmesan cheese over top. Bake in 350°F. oven 30 to 45 minutes. Serve from baking dish.

14 · Satisfying Salads

When is a salad not a tossed salad? When it is encased in shimmering gelatin with ingredients scattered throughout; then it is called a "mold." If the word mold conjures up thoughts of the color green, be assured that gelatin salad molds can be made in assorted colors and contents—including green. Three good rules for successful molds that slip out of their forms easily and hold their shape:

1. Lightly oil the form with a good grade of salad oil, draining the form upside down to remove excess oil.

2. Be stingy with the liquid that you add.

3. Be generous with the other ingredients that you add.

Following these rules will give you a head start on producing a dish that will not plop all over the platter. To remove the mold after it is firmly refrigerated, dip it up to its rim in warm water and quickly invert on a serving dish. If it stubbornly resists sliding out, dip it again.

When preparing tossed salads, take the time to crisp the salad greens before you serve them. There's nothing appetizing about soggy lettuce!

Wash greens thoroughly and discard those leaves that are discolored or too limp for use. Drain dry and wrap in paper toweling, then refrigerate in the crisper compartment until you are ready to tear it up for your salad.

Scrape carrots and trim celery about a half hour before serving, and then plunge them into ice water until needed. You'll guarantee crunchy texture every time.

Be adventurous with salads. Don't be afraid to toss in a few leftover bits of vegetables that you cooked the night before—they take on a new taste when they are served in a cold salad. At another time you might want to add some apple wedges or other fruit sections, and don't forget that nuts enhance a salad too.

Keep freeze-dried chives on your spice and herb rack, and sprinkle a tablespoon or two over your greens to give them a faint onion flavor. And for special moments, toss in the contents of a jar of artichoke hearts, oil and all.

ANTIPASTO SALAD

To serve 6 to 8:

AMOUNT	INGREDIENTS
1 pound	Large shell macaroni, cooked and drained
12 slices	Hard salami, cut in thin strips
4-ounce package	Sliced Genoa salami, cut in thin strips
6-ounce package	Sliced processed Swiss cheese, cut in thin strips
1/4 cup	Diced green onion
1/2 cup	Diced green pepper
1 cup	Diced celery
1 cup	Cherry tomatoes, sliced in half
1 cup	Whole pitted ripe olives
1 teaspoon	Salt
1/4 teaspoon	Black pepper
1/4 cup	Italian-style salad dressing

Cook the shell macaroni according to package directions; drain and rinse with cold water to separate the shells; drain again. In a large salad bowl, combine all the ingredients and toss lightly with Italian dressing. Garnish with extra ripe olives if desired.

CAESAR SALAD

| *To serve 2 or 3:* | *To serve 4 to 6:* | |
AMOUNT	AMOUNT	INGREDIENTS
1 clove	1 clove	Garlic, peeled
1 head	2 heads	Romaine lettuce
1/2 can	1 can (2-ounce)	Anchovies
3 tablespoons	6 tablespoons	Olive oil
1/4 teaspoon	1/2 teaspoon	Salt
1/8 teaspoon	1/4 teaspoon	Black pepper
2 tablespoons	1/4 cup	Lemon juice
1/2 cup	1 cup	Garlic-flavored croutons
1	2	Coddled eggs
2 tablespoons	1/4 cup	Grated Parmesan cheese

Rub salad bowl thoroughly with garlic, then discard garlic. Tear chilled lettuce into bite-size pieces. Mash anchovies into olive oil; add salt, pepper, and lemon juice. Pour over greens. Add coddled eggs and toss. *(To coddle eggs:* Boil water and remove from heat. Immerse eggs for two minutes. Remove from water and crack open.) Sprinkle cheese over all and toss again. Serve at once.

CHINESE BEAN SALAD

To serve 2 or 3:	To serve 4 to 6:	
AMOUNT	AMOUNT	INGREDIENTS
1 can (16-ounce)	2 cans	Diagonal-cut green beans, drained
1/2 can	1 can (5-ounce)	Water chestnuts, drained and sliced
1/2	1	Red onion, sliced thin
3 tablespoons	6 tablespoons	Sugar
3 tablespoons	6 tablespoons	Wine vinegar
1 tablespoon	2 tablespoons	Salad oil
1 tablespoon	2 tablespoons	Soy sauce
1/4 teaspoon	1/2 teaspoon	Celery salt

Combine beans, water chestnuts, and onion rings in a large bowl. Dissolve sugar in vinegar, add salad oil, soy sauce, and celery salt; stir briskly and pour over beans. Chill several hours or overnight, stirring occasionally.

SWISS-FLAVORED WALDORF SALAD

To serve 2 or 3:	To serve 4 to 6:	
AMOUNT	AMOUNT	INGREDIENTS
1 small head	1 large head	Chilled lettuce
1	2	Apples, diced
1 1/2 tablespoons	3 tablespoons	Lemon juice
2 tablespoons	1/4 cup	Seedless raisins
2 tablespoons	1/4 cup	Grated Swiss cheese
2 tablespoons	1/4 cup	Mayonnaise
2 tablespoons	1/4 cup	Dairy sour cream

Shred lettuce into a salad bowl. Stir diced apples with lemon juice to prevent browning; add to lettuce with raisins and Swiss cheese. Combine mayonnaise and sour cream; Pour over salad just before serving.

PINEAPPLE-COCONUT SALAD WITH GOLDEN DRESSING

To serve 2 or 3:	*To serve 4 to 6:*	
AMOUNT (SALAD)	AMOUNT (SALAD)	INGREDIENTS
1 small head	1 large head	Chilled lettuce
1 can (8-ounce)	1 can (1-pound)	Crushed pineapple, drain and reserve syrup
1 cup	2 cups	Sliced celery
1/2 cup	1 cup	Shredded coconut
AMOUNT (DRESSING)	AMOUNT (DRESSING)	
1/4 cup	1/2 cup	Pineapple juice drained from above crushed pineapple
1 1/2 teaspoons	1 tablespoon	Sugar
1 1/2 teaspoons	1 tablespoon	Lemon juice
1 1/2 teaspoons	1 tablespoon	Salad oil
1 teaspoon	2 teaspoons	Prepared yellow mustard
1/4 teaspoon	1/2 teaspoon	Salt

Toss shredded lettuce, drained pineapple, celery, and coconut together. Combine pineapple juice, sugar, lemon juice, oil, mustard, and salt; mix thoroughly and pour over mixed greens and fruit just before serving.

CORN RELISH SALAD

To serve 4 to 6:

AMOUNT	INGREDIENTS
1 can (12-ounce)	Whole kernel corn, drained
1/4 cup	Sweet pickle relish, well drained
1/2 cup	Sliced black olives
1/2 cup	Sliced celery
1 teaspoon	Salt
2 tablespoons	Sugar
2 tablespoons	Wine vinegar
6 tablespoons	Salad oil
1 head	Lettuce, shredded

Combine corn, pickle relish, olives, and celery. Dissolve salt and sugar in vinegar; add salad oil and stir briskly. Pour over corn mixture. Chill several hours, stirring occasionally. When ready to serve, add lettuce and toss lightly to mix.

This vegetable salad can be prepared ahead of time. If there's any left over, refrigerate and serve the next day. It's an appealing combination for those days when lettuce turns you off.

TANGY VEGETABLE SALAD

To serve 3 to 4:	To serve 6 to 8:	
AMOUNT	AMOUNT	INGREDIENTS
1/4 cup	1/2 cup	Dairy sour cream
1 1/2 teaspoons	1 tablespoon	Sugar
1 teaspoon	2 teaspoons	Cider vinegar
1/2 teaspoon	1 teaspoon	Dill weed
1/4 teaspoon	1/2 teaspoon	Salt
1/8 teaspoon	1/4 teaspoon	Prepared mustard
Dash	Dash	Black pepper
1/2 package	1 package (10-ounce)	Frozen peas
3/4 cup	1 1/2 cups	Shredded Cheddar cheese
1	2	Hard-cooked eggs, chopped
1/4 cup	1/2 cup	Chopped sweet pickle
1/4 cup	1/2 cup	Thinly sliced celery
1/4 cup	1/2 cup	Sliced radishes

Prepare dressing by combining sour cream, sugar, vinegar, dill weed, salt, mustard, and pepper. Cover and chill. Cook peas according to package directions; drain and chill. To assemble salad, combine peas, cheese, eggs, pickle, celery, and radishes. Toss with dressing.

Are you especially fond of blue cheese? Then here's a cole slaw recipe that includes blue cheese in the dressing. Delightfully different!

BLUE CHEESE SLAW

To serve 3 or 4:	*To serve 6 to 8:*	
AMOUNT	AMOUNT	INGREDIENTS
3 cups	6 cups	Shredded cabbage
1 tablespoon	2 tablespoons	Chopped green onion
1/2 cup	1 cup	Crumbled blue cheese
1/4 cup	1/2 cup	Dairy sour cream
1 tablespoon	2 tablespoons	Light cream (or half-and-half)
1 1/2 teaspoons	1 tablespoon	Lemon juice
1/4 teaspoon	1/2 teaspoon	Sugar
Dash	1/8 teaspoon	Salt

In a large bowl combine cabbage and onion; chill thoroughly. In a small mixing bowl beat together blue cheese, sour cream, cream, lemon juice, sugar, and salt. Just before serving add dressing to cabbage; toss lightly.

ESROM SLAW

To serve 2 or 3:	*To serve 4 to 6:*	
AMOUNT	AMOUNT	INGREDIENTS
2 cups	4 cups	Shredded cabbage
1/4 cup	1/2 cup	Diced Esrom cheese
1 teaspoon	2 teaspoons	Minced onion
1/4 cup	1/2 cup	Mayonnaise
2 tablespoons	1/4 cup	Salad oil
1 tablespoon	2 tablespoons	Wine vinegar
1/4 teaspoon	1/2 teaspoon	Salt
1/8 teaspoon	1/4 teaspoon	Pepper

Place shredded cabbage in a bowl; add Esrom cheese. Combine onion, mayonnaise, oil, vinegar, salt, and pepper; pour over cabbage and toss well. Refrigerate until ready to serve.

POTATO SALAD

To serve 2 or 3:	To serve 4 to 6:	
AMOUNT	AMOUNT	INGREDIENTS
2 or 3	4 to 6	Cooked, peeled potatoes
1 small	1 large	Onion, sliced thin
1 tablespoon	2 tablespoons	Parsley, chopped
1	2	Hard-cooked eggs, diced
1/4 cup	1/2 cup	Celery, diced fine
1/4 cup	1/2 cup	Mayonnaise
1/4 cup	1/2 cup	Dairy sour cream
1 teaspoon	2 teaspoons	Lemon juice
1/2 teaspoon	1 teaspoon	Sugar
1/4 teaspoon	1/2 teaspoon	Salt

Cut potatoes into chunks; add onion, parsley, eggs, and celery. Stir together mayonnaise, sour cream, lemon juice, sugar, and salt. Pour over potatoes and stir thoroughly. Chill until ready to serve.

Serve Orange Cream Salad Mold surrounded with fresh fruits and use it for a main dish on hot summer days. Made with sour cream, cottage cheese, and Cheddar cheese, it is a high protein delight.

ORANGE CREAM SALAD MOLD

To make 6 servings:

AMOUNT	INGREDIENTS
3/4 cup	Orange juice
1 package (3-ounce)	Orange-flavored gelatin
1 cup	Cottage cheese
1 cup	Dairy sour cream
3/4 cup	Finely chopped celery
1/2 cup	Shredded Cheddar cheese
2 tablespoons	Lemon juice

Heat orange juice to boiling point; pour over gelatin in small mixing bowl and stir until gelatin is dissolved. Chill until mixture is the consistency of unbeaten egg white. Beat gelatin mixture about 5 minutes. Fold in cottage cheese, sour cream, celery, Cheddar cheese, and lemon juice; turn into a 5-cup salad mold. Chill until firm. Unmold and serve garnished with fresh fruit, if desired.

LIME SALAD MOLD

To serve 6 to 8:

AMOUNT	INGREDIENTS
1 package (6-ounce)	Lime-flavored gelatin
2 cups	Boiling water
1 1/2 cups	Cold water
1 1/2 cups	Finely shredded cabbage
1 1/2 cups	Finely shredded carrots
1/4 cup	Diced pimiento

Empty contents of gelatin package into a large bowl. Add boiling water and stir until gelatin is completely dissolved. Add cold water and stir again. Add cabbage, carrots, and diced pimiento. Pour into a ring mold. Refrigerate until firm, at least 6 hours. Unmold, and serve in place of a salad, or as part of a buffet table.

CRANBERRY FRUIT SALAD

To serve 6 to 8:

AMOUNT	INGREDIENTS
2 tablespoons	Unflavored gelatin
2 cups	Cranberry juice cocktail
2 cups	Apple juice
2 tablespoons	Lemon juice
1 can (1-pound)	Whole cranberry sauce
1	Apple, diced
1 cup	Broken walnuts

Sprinkle gelatin over ½ cup cranberry juice. Let stand 5 minutes to soften. Stir over low heat until gelatin is dissolved. Add remaining cranberry juice, apple juice, and lemon juice. Blend well. Add cranberry sauce and apple; stir until cranberry sauce is distributed evenly throughout, then add nuts. Pour mixture into 2-quart mold. Chill until firm, at least 6 hours. Unmold and garnish with crisp salad greens.

PINEAPPLE MOLD

To serve 6 to 8:

AMOUNT	INGREDIENTS
1 can (29-ounce)	Sliced pineapple
1 package (3-ounce)	Lime-flavored gelatin
1/2 cup	Boiling water

Drain pineapple juice into a measuring cup, but leave slices intact in the can. Empty gelatin into a bowl; add boiling water and stir briskly to dissolve gelatin. Add water to the juice until it measures 1¼ cups; stir this into the gelatin mixture. Pour gelatin mixture back into the can of pineapple and chill until firm. To serve, puncture bottom of can and slide molded pineapple out onto a platter. Slice between the pineapple slices and serve.

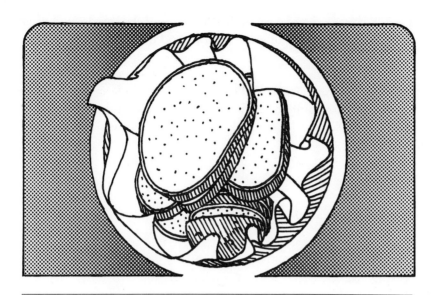

15 · Easy Bread

Sometimes "the staff of life" can become the life of the party just by being hot, fragrant, and delicious. In your busy life it is unlikely that you will have time to mix yeast dough and bake your own bread, but there are many new bread ideas that you can adapt quickly into specialties of your own.

Next time you are in the market, examine the brown-and-serve breads that can be refrigerated or frozen until you need them. Snoop around the cake mixes and see how many quick-mix breads with delicate fruit-and-nut flavorings are just waiting for your approval. In the refrigerated section you will find tubes of marvelous biscuits, crescent rolls, and rolls of many other shapes, all waiting to be popped in the oven for ten to twenty minutes and then to emerge freshly baked and delicious. The freezer section too, has baked and frozen breads and rolls that need a mere thawing, or possibly a browning and baking, before serving.

Naturally, you will not want to overlook the French and Italian loaves of fresh bread at the bakery counter. These are always a taste treat, but even more so when they are slit and slathered with butter and garlic, or minced onion, or herbs, and then heated just before serving.

All the recipes in this chapter are based on these quick breads that you can buy for a start. Then little tricks are described to show you how to adventure away from the directions on the package and produce bread that is uniquely your own. Try them and see how easy it is.

HOT GARLIC BREAD

To serve 6 to 8:

AMOUNT	INGREDIENTS
1 large loaf	French bread
1/4 cup	Melted butter
1 clove	Garlic, finely minced

Cut French bread in ¾-inch slices on the diagonal, almost but not all the way through to the bottom. Stir garlic into melted butter; brush this mixture liberally between the slices. Wrap in aluminum foil and heat in 400°F. oven for 10 to 15 minutes. This may be arranged earlier in the day, wrapped in foil, and refrigerated until ready for the oven.

BARBECUED FRENCH BREAD

To serve 6 to 8:

AMOUNT	INGREDIENTS
1/3 cup	Chopped onions
1/2 clove	Garlic, minced
2 tablespoons	Butter
1/3 cup	Chili sauce
1 1/2 teaspoons	Tabasco sauce
2 tablespoons	Vinegar
1 tablespoon	Prepared mustard
1 large loaf	French bread
1 tablespoon	Grated Parmesan cheese

Sauté onion and garlic in butter; add chili sauce, Tabasco, vinegar, brown sugar, and prepared mustard. Simmer over low heat until mixture thickens, about 5 minutes, stirring constantly. Cut French bread in ¾-inch slices on the diagonal, almost but not all the way through to the bottom. Spread sauce between slices; sprinkle with Parmesan cheese. Wrap in aluminum foil and heat in 400°F. oven for 15 minutes. This may be arranged earlier in the day, wrapped in foil, and refrigerated until ready for the oven.

ORANGE-NUT BISCUITS

To make 10 biscuits:

AMOUNT	INGREDIENTS
1 package (8-ounce)	Refrigerator biscuits in a tube
1/4 cup	Frozen orange juice concentrate, thawed and undiluted
3 tablespoons	Chopped nuts
3 tablespoons	Brown sugar

Place biscuits in ungreased 8- or 9-inch round pan. Bake according to package directions. Combine orange juice concentrate, nuts, and brown sugar. Spoon over biscuits. Bake 4 to 5 minutes longer. Serve at once.

SESAME SEED BISCUITS

To make 10 biscuits:

AMOUNT	INGREDIENTS
1 package	Refrigerator biscuits in a tube
1 tablespoon	Melted butter
2 tablespoons	Sesame seeds

Separate 10 biscuits, brush with melted butter, and roll in sesame seeds. Place on a cookie sheet and bake in a 400°F. oven for 10 to 15 minutes, or until biscuits are golden. Serve hot.

CINNAMON WHEELS

To make 10 rolls:

AMOUNT	INGREDIENTS
1 package	Refrigerator biscuits in a tube
1/4 cup	Brown sugar
1/2 teaspoon	Cinnamon
2 tablespoons	Melted butter

Separate biscuits and roll each flat to ⅛-inch thickness. Combine sugar, cinnamon, and melted butter. Spread each biscuit with some of this mixture and roll up, jelly-roll fashion. Grease a muffin tin and fill each cup with a rolled biscuit by coiling it into a circle. Bake in a 400°F. oven for 10 to 15 minutes, or until the rolls are golden. Serve hot.

ORANGE-NUT CRESCENTS

To make 8 rolls:

AMOUNT	INGREDIENTS
1 package	Refrigerator crescent rolls in a tube
1/4 cup	Orange marmalade
1/4 cup	Chopped walnuts

Separate rolls and carefully unroll each. Spread each triangle with a mixture of marmalade and walnuts; roll into a crescent shape, starting with the wide end and rolling to the point. Place on a greased baking sheet and bake at 375°F. for 12 to 15 minutes, or until golden brown. Serve warm.

ONION CRESCENTS

To make 8 rolls:

AMOUNT	INGREDIENTS
1 package	Refrigerator crescent rolls in a tube
1/4 cup	Dairy sour cream
1 tablespoon	Dried onion soup mix

Separate rolls and carefully unroll each. Spread each triangle with a mixture of sour cream and onion soup mix; roll into a crescent shape, starting with the wide end and rolling to the point. Place on a greased baking sheet and bake at 375°F. for 12 to 15 minutes, or until golden brown. Serve warm.

MOLASSES BRAN MUFFINS

To make 12 small muffins:

AMOUNT	INGREDIENTS
1/4 cup	Shortening
1/4 cup	Molasses
1	Egg
1 cup	Bran
3/4 cup	Milk
1 cup	Sifted flour
2 1/2 teaspoons	Baking powder
1/2 teaspoon	Salt
1/2 cup	Finely cut dates

Blend together shortening and molasses. Add egg; beat well. Stir in bran and milk; let stand until most of moisture is absorbed. Sift together flour, baking powder and salt. Add to molasses mixture with dates; stir only until blended. Fill greased muffin pans ⅔ full. Bake in a 350°F. oven for 30 minutes.

Wheat Germ Prune Bread, sweetened with honey, has a pleasantly coarse texture that boasts of chunks of pitted prunes. Just right for this revival age of bread-baking for good health.

WHEAT GERM PRUNE BREAD

To make 16 two-inch square servings:

AMOUNT	INGREDIENTS
2 1/4 cups	Sifted all-purpose flour
1 1/2 cups	Wheat germ
2 teaspoons	Baking powder
1 teaspoon	Baking soda
1 1/2 teaspoons	Salt
1/2 cup	Butter
1 package (12-ounce)	Pitted prunes, snipped in small pieces
2	Eggs
3/4 cup	Honey
3/4 cup	Milk

Combine flour, wheat germ, baking powder, baking soda, and salt. Cut in butter with fork until mixture looks like coarse oatmeal. Stir in prunes. Add eggs, one at a time, mixing well after each. Add milk and honey all at once and combine well. Turn batter into greased 8-inch-square pan and bake in preheated 350°F. oven for 35 to 45 minutes, or until pick inserted in center comes out clean.

Here's another prune bread—this time using nutritious whole wheat flour and nuts. Spread with softened cream cheese for a tasty treat.

WHOLE WHEAT PRUNE-NUT LOAF

To make a 9-inch by 5-inch loaf:

AMOUNT	INGREDIENTS
1 1/4 cups	Sifted all-purpose flour
1 teaspoon	Baking powder
1 teaspoon	Baking soda
1 teaspoon	Salt
1/2 cup	Sugar
1 1/2 cups	Whole wheat flour
1 cup	Finely snipped pitted prunes
1 cup	Chopped walnuts
1	Lemon, grated rind and juice
1	Egg, beaten
1 1/4 cups	Milk
1/2 cup	Melted butter
1/4 cup	Molasses

Sift flour, baking powder, baking soda, salt, and sugar together into a large bowl. Add whole wheat flour, prunes, walnuts, and lemon rind. Combine thoroughly. Make a well in the center and add lemon juice, egg, milk, butter, and molasses. Stir well, slowly working in surrounding dry ingredients. Mix just until all ingredients are combined; do not overbeat. Put batter into well greased 9-inch by 5-inch loaf pan. Bake in a preheated 350°F. oven for 60 to 70 minutes, or until pick inserted in center comes out clean.

16 · Deceptive Desserts

When you are in a hurry or on a diet, you have several options at the dessert course level—including "skip it" or "buy it." But there are other times when you want to putter in the kitchen and produce something worthy of the name "dessert."

This chapter presents you with a gamut of recipes for just those moments. Some start with ice cream and are shaped with a mold or showered with fruit; others start with fruit that is chilled and sauced; and still others provide you with directions for baking a cake that you can nibble on for days afterward. All have been selected because of their easy qualities and satisfying tastes.

If you keep a few toppings on your pantry shelf, such as a can of coconut, nuts, chocolate bits, and syrup, you can always turn ice cream into a tempting sundae. Two or three kinds of canned fruit halves can be combined, with a little cinnamon added, to produce a respectable fruit compote. And a cake mix can always be stirred up into a quick but satisfying cake—examine the package before purchase to be sure that it is uncomplicated, and choose a name brand that stands for excellence. If you have a particular craving for cake at the end of every meal, you can keep yourself well and economically supplied by baking one cake on the weekend and another during the middle of the week. Don't overlook the interesting icings that are all ready in a can in many flavors, and in packages that need only water to stir into spreadable frosting.

Many puddings and gelatins are also available, to give you variety and keep your sweet tooth tingling. And try the no-cook pie fillings poured into a pan lined with split lady fingers. Little mixing is involved in any of these, and your refrigerator does the rest.

If you have a super-important dinner to serve and no time to think about making the dessert yourself, when money is not of prime consideration, serve a platter of assorted French pastries from a good local bakery. Let each guest choose his or her own favorite, and provide extras for duplicate tastes. Be sure to keep those with whipped cream well chilled to prevent spoilage.

Dessert is a time to relax and enjoy the final curtain of the meal. Whatever you select to serve, be sure that the coffee or tea that accompanies it is delicious too.

If you are lucky enough to have an electric chafing dish or fondue pot, use it for the delicious Cherries Jubilee. Keep it warm over hot water until serving time, then spoon it over vanilla ice cream and bow to the expected applause.

CHERRIES JUBILEE

To serve 4 or 5:	To serve 8 to 10:	
AMOUNT	AMOUNT	INGREDIENTS
1 can (1 pound)	2 cans	Dark, sweet pitted cherries
Thin rind of 1/8	Thin rind of 1/4	Lemon, shredded
2 tablespoons	1/4 cup	Sugar
1 tablespoon	2 tablespoons	Cornstarch
1 teaspoon	2 teaspoons	Lemon juice
2 tablespoons	1/4 cup	Cointreau
2 tablespoons	1/4 cup	Brandy

Drain syrup from cherries; mix lemon rind, sugar, and cornstarch until smooth. Heat until thickened, stirring constantly. Reduce heat; add lemon juice, Cointreau, and cherries. Keep warm over hot water until serving time. To serve, heat brandy in a small saucepan, pour over cherries and ignite. Spoon over individual servings of ice cream.

MAPLE SYRUP MOUSSE WITH STRAWBERRIES

To serve 6:

AMOUNT	INGREDIENTS
1 envelope	Unflavored gelatin
3/4 cup	Water
1 cup	Maple syrup
Dash	Salt
1 cup	Heavy cream, whipped
1 pint	Fresh strawberries, sliced
4 tablespoons	Sugar

Soften gelatin in water in a small saucepan, then stir over low heat until dissolved. Blend gelatin mixture with maple syrup and salt in a bowl; chill until mixture mounds slightly when dropped from a spoon. Fold in whipped cream. Pour into a 1-quart serving dish or compote. Chill until set. Meanwhile, combine strawberries and 3 tablespoons of the sugar; chill. Serve the mousse topped with the strawberries, sprinkled with the remaining tablespoon of sugar.

STRAWBERRY MOUSSE

To make 6 to 8 servings:

AMOUNT	INGREDIENTS
1 pint	Fresh sliced strawberries
1/2 cup	Sugar
1 package (3-ounce)	Strawberry-flavored gelatin
1 pint	Vanilla ice cream
1/2 cup	Flaked coconut
1/2 cup	Finely chopped pecans

In a bowl toss sugar and strawberries; let stand at room temperature at least 1 hour, tossing occasionally; drain and reserve juice. Add sufficient water to reserved strawberry juice to make 1 cup; bring to boiling. In a bowl, pour this boiling strawberry liquid over the gelatin; stir until dissolved. Spoon ice cream into hot gelatin mixture; stir until melted. Cool. When partially thickened, whip in a mixing bowl at highest speed for about 2 minutes. Fold in strawberries, coconut, and pecans. Pour into a 4-cup mold; chill until firm. Garnish with additional strawberries, if desired, just before serving.

The simplest and perhaps the best way to serve fresh strawberries is sugared, chilled, and served in a tall, stemmed glass. Pour dry white wine over all—or try the sweet cream and sour cream combinations that follow.

STRAWBERRIES WITH SWEET CREAM

To serve 2 or 3:	*To serve 4 to 6:*	
AMOUNT	AMOUNT	INGREDIENTS
1 pint	2 pints	Fresh strawberries, washed, hulled, and halved
3 tablespoons	6 tablespoons	Confectioners' sugar
1/2 cup	1 cup	Heavy cream
1/4 teaspoon	1/2 teaspoon	Vanilla
1 tablespoon	2 tablespoons	Lemon juice
Sprigs	Sprigs	Fresh mint (optional)

Chill strawberries with ½ of the sugar for about 20 minutes. Whip the cream with remaining sugar and vanilla, adding lemon juice as you finish. Pile strawberries into parfait glasses or serving dishes; top with whipped cream and the sprigs of mint.

STRAWBERRIES WITH SOUR CREAM

To serve 2 or 3:	*To serve 4 to 6:*	
AMOUNT	AMOUNT	INGREDIENTS
1 pint	2 pints	Fresh strawberries
1 cup	1 pint	Dairy sour cream
3 tablespoons	6 tablespoons	Dark brown sugar
1/2 teaspoon	1 teaspoon	Vanilla
1 teaspoon	2 teaspoons	Lemon juice

Wash strawberries, leaving them whole and unhulled. For a dipping sauce, blend sour cream, brown sugar, vanilla, and lemon juice together until smooth. Serve strawberries on a platter with dipping sauce in the center for a do-it-yourself dessert.

For an elegant but easy dinner dessert, choose Banana Cup Véronique. Place a decorative cocktail pick in each glass so that the fruit can be nibbled while sipping the wine.

BANANA CUP VÉRONIQUE

To serve each portion:

AMOUNT	INGREDIENTS
1/2	Ripe banana, peeled
4	Seedless grapes
4 ounces	White port wine, chilled (or ginger ale, chilled)

Slice banana and place in a stemmed wine glass. Add washed grapes. Pour chilled wine over fruit and serve at once.

FRUIT WITH COCONUT SAUCE

To serve 4:

AMOUNT	INGREDIENTS
2 cups	Diced fresh (or drained canned) fruits
1 cup	Dairy sour cream
2 tablespoons	Brown sugar
1/2 cup	Flaked coconut

Mix fruit in a bowl; set aside. Combine sour cream and brown sugar; stir until sugar is dissolved. Fold in coconut. Place fruit mixture in 4 individual dessert dishes. Spoon about ¼ cup coconut sauce on each dessert. Sprinkle with additional coconut, if desired.

PEACH ROMANOFF

To serve 3 or 4:	*To serve 6 to 8:*	
AMOUNT	AMOUNT	INGREDIENTS
1 package (12-ounce)	2 packages	Frozen peach slices, thawed and drained
3 tablespoons	6 tablespoons	Cointreau
1/4 cup	1/2 cup	Evaporated milk
1 tablespoon	2 tablespoons	Lemon juice
1 pint	1 quart	Peach ice cream, softened

Mix peaches and Cointreau and let stand. Chill evaporated milk in ice tray until almost frozen at edges. Chill small bowl and beaters of mixer. Remove ice-cold milk from ice tray into chilled bowl and beat until fluffy. Add lemon juice and whip until stiff. Beat ice cream in a larger bowl until creamy. Add peach and whipped milk mixtures. Beat at low speed just until mixed. Serve in chilled dessert dishes. May be kept in freezer up to 1 hour.

Use your chafing dish or electric skillet for this quick but elegant dessert, and cook it right at the table. Top-of-the-range skillet cooking is fine too.

BANANA FLAMBÉ

To serve 4:

AMOUNT	INGREDIENTS
2 tablespoons	**Butter**
1/2 cup	**Sugar**
1/2 cup	**Port wine**
1/2 cup	**Red currant jelly**
2 tablespoons	**Slivered candied ginger**
1/2	**Lemon, grated rind and juice**
4	**Bananas, cut in half crosswise**
4 slices	**Canned pineapple, drained**
1 can (11-ounce)	**Mandarin oranges, drained**
1/4 cup	**Brandy, heated**
1/4 cup	**Flaked coconut (fresh or packaged)**

Melt butter in blazer of chafing dish or large skillet. Add sugar, wine, jelly, ginger, lemon rind, and juice to butter and stir until well blended. Add bananas, pineapple, and oranges and simmer 4 to 5 minutes, basting the sauce over the fruits to form a glaze. Just before serving, heat the brandy and pour it over the fruits. Ignite. Sprinkle each serving with coconut.

You'll never bomb with an ice cream bombe—or mold—for dessert! All you need is a fluted 1-quart mold and a few ingredients to make it interesting.

APRICOT ICE CREAM MOLD

To serve 6:

AMOUNT	INGREDIENTS
1/2 cup	**Apricot preserves**
1/2 cup	**Sliced toasted almonds**
1 quart	**Vanilla ice cream, softened**

Chill a 1-quart mold in the freezer. In a small bowl combine preserves and almonds. Press into bottom and part-way up the sides of mold. Freeze until firm. Press ice cream into mold. Return to freezer to harden. To unmold, dip into warm water and turn out onto chilled plate. Return to freezer to harden until serving time.

CHERRY ICE CREAM PIE

To serve 6 to 8:

AMOUNT (CRUST)	INGREDIENTS
1 1/3 cups	**Vanilla wafer crumbs**
2 tablespoons	**Sugar**
1/4 cup	**Butter, melted**
1 teaspoon	**Almond extract**

AMOUNT (FILLING)	INGREDIENTS
1 quart	**Vanilla ice cream**
1 can (1-pound 5-ounce)	**Cherry pie filling**
1 cup	**Whipping cream**
2 tablespoons	**Confectioners' sugar**
1/2 teaspoon	**Vanilla**
2 tablespoons	**Toasted sliced almonds**

To prepare crust: In a small bowl mix together crumbs and sugar; stir in melted butter and almond extract. Press mixture firmly and evenly against bottom and sides of a 9-inch pie plate, building up slightly around rim. Bake in a preheated 350°F. oven for 5 minutes. Cool on wire rack. Chill crust, in freezer if possible.

To prepare filling: Soften ice cream very slightly; spade into crust alternating 1 cup of cherry pie filling with ice cream. Return to freezer to harden. About 10 minutes before serving, remove pie from freezer to soften slightly. Meanwhile, whip cream until almost stiff; add confectioners' sugar and vanilla; continue beating until very stiff. Gently fold in remaining cup of cherry pie filling. Spread top of pie with cherry-whip cream. Sprinkle with almonds.

APPLE RIPPLE PARFAITS

To serve 3 or 4:	To serve 6 to 8:	
AMOUNT	AMOUNT	INGREDIENTS
3/4 cup	1 1/2 cups	Canned apple sauce
1/4 cup	1/2 cup	Brown sugar
1/4 teaspoon	1/2 teaspoon	Cinnamon
1/4 teaspoon	1/2 teaspoon	Grated lemon rind
1/4 cup	1/2 cup	Chopped walnuts
1 pint	1 quart	Softened ice cream

Combine apple sauce, brown sugar, cinnamon, lemon rind, and walnuts. Swirl through softened ice cream. Pour into parfait glasses or freezer tray and freeze. Serve slightly softened.

EASY BAVARIAN

To serve 8 to 12:	
AMOUNT	INGREDIENTS
1 package (6-ounce)	Black cherry-flavored gelatin
2 cups	Boiling water
2 cans (13 ounces each)	Evaporated milk
1 teaspoon	Almond extract
1 tablespoon	Lemon juice

Dissolve gelatin in boiling water. Gradually blend in evaporated milk. Add almond extract and lemon juice. Chill until thickened but not firm. Place bowl of gelatin mixture in a large bowl of ice and water. Whip gelatin mixture until fluffy and thick. Pour into a 2-quart glass serving dish and chill until firm. To serve, spoon portions of Bavarian onto plates at the table.

PINEAPPLE SHERRY GELATIN

To serve 4:

AMOUNT	INGREDIENTS
1 package (3-ounce)	Lemon-flavored gelatin
1 cup	Boiling water
1 can (8 3/4-ounce)	Pineapple tidbits
1/4 cup	Dry sherry wine
1 cup	Commercially prepared whipped topping

Dissolve gelatin in boiling water. Drain pineapple, reserving syrup. Add water to syrup to make ½ cup. Add measured liquid and wine to gelatin mixture. Chill until thickened. Stir in pineapple tidbits. Pour into individual dessert glasses. Chill until firm—at least 4 hours. Top with prepared whipped topping.

CREAMY ORANGE-PINEAPPLE MOLD

To serve 8 to 10:

AMOUNT	INGREDIENTS
2 tablespoons (2 envelopes)	Unflavored gelatin
1/2 cup	Cold water
1 can (1-pound 4 1/2-ounce)	Crushed pineapple, undrained
2/3 cup	Orange juice
1/3 cup	Lemon juice
1/3 cup	Sugar
2 cups	Dairy sour cream
2 cups	Sliced strawberries
1/2 cup	Chopped pecans

In a saucepan, sprinkle gelatin over water to soften. Heat over low heat, stirring constantly until gelatin is dissolved. Stir in pineapple with syrup, orange and lemon juices, and sugar; stir until sugar is dissolved. Pour into a large bowl; chill until jelly-like in consistency. Stir sour cream into gelatin mixture; fold in strawberries and nuts. Turn into a 7-cup mold; chill until set.

For a fluffy dessert that will satisfy every sweet tooth at your party, decide to make Marshmallow Fruit Cream Squares. It goes together in minutes, yet looks as if you have spent hours in the preparation. A tasty trick, this one!

MARSHMALLOW FRUIT CREAM SQUARES

To serve 8 to 10:

AMOUNT	INGREDIENTS
2 2/3 cups	Vanilla wafer crumbs (about 60 wafers)
1/2 cup	Melted butter
1 package (1-pound)	Marshmallows
1 cup	Milk
1 cup	Dairy sour cream
1/2 teaspoon	Cinnamon
1/4 teaspoon	Nutmeg
1 can (20-ounce)	Fruit salad, well drained
1/2 cup	Toasted, salted sliced almonds

In a bowl mix together crumbs and butter. Press mixture firmly and evenly against bottom and sides of a shallow 2-quart flat-bottomed baking dish. Chill. Meanwhile, in a large saucepan heat marshmallows and milk over low heat; stir occasionally, until marshmallows are melted. Cool to room temperature; stir to blend thoroughly. Fold in sour cream, cinnamon, and nutmeg. Combine fruit and toasted almonds; fold into marshmallow mixture. Pour into crumb crust. Cover and chill until firm. Cut in squares to serve.

What can you do with day-old bread? Here's a nourishing dessert with the delicious richness of chocolate, milk, and eggs. Who would guess that underneath its glamour lies the makings of old-fashioned bread pudding!

CHOCOLATE BREAD PUDDING

To serve 3 or 4:	*To serve 6 to 8:*	
AMOUNT	AMOUNT	INGREDIENTS
1 cup	2 cups	Milk
1 square (1-ounce)	2 squares	Semi-sweet baking chocolate
2	4	Eggs, slightly beaten
1/4 cup	1/2 cup	Sugar
1/2 teaspoon	1 teaspoon	Vanilla
Dash	Dash or two	Salt
4 or 5 slices	8 to 10 slices	Day-old bread, cut in cubes

In a large saucepan heat milk and chocolate over medium heat, stirring occasionally, until chocolate is melted. Blend a small amount of hot mixture into beaten eggs; return the egg mixture to the saucepan along with sugar, vanilla, and salt. Stir until blended. Add bread cubes; mix well. Pour into a buttered casserole. Set casserole in a shallow pan on oven rack; pour hot water into pan around casserole 1 inch deep. Bake in preheated 350°F. oven for 35 minutes, or until a knife inserted near center comes out clean. Remove from water and allow to cool partially on wire rack. Spoon out on dessert plates and top with dollops of Orange Cream (below).

ORANGE CREAM

To serve 3 or 4:	*To serve 6 to 8:*	
AMOUNT	AMOUNT	INGREDIENTS
1/4 cup	1/2 cup	Dairy sour cream
1 tablespoon	2 tablespoons	Confectioners' sugar
1/8 teaspoon	1/4 teaspoon	Grated orange rind
1 tablespoon	2 tablespoons	Orange juice

Combine ingredients and use as a topping for Chocolate Bread Pudding (above).

BREAD PUDDING

To serve 2 or 3:	To serve 4 to 6:	
AMOUNT	AMOUNT	INGREDIENTS
1 heaping cup	2 1/4 cups	Bread cubes
1/4 cup	1/2 cup	Raisins
Dash	1/8 teaspoon	Salt
1	2	Eggs
1 1/4 cups	2 1/2 cups	Milk
2 tablespoons	1/4 cup	Molasses
1 1/2 teaspoons	1 tablespoon	Butter
2 tablespoons	2 tablespoons	Sugar
1/4 teaspoon	1/4 teaspoon	Cinnamon

Combine bread cubes and raisins in a casserole; sprinkle with salt. Beat together eggs and milk; blend in molasses. Stir into bread mixture; dot with butter. Combine sugar and cinnamon; sprinkle evenly over top. Bake in a moderate oven of 350°F. for 30 to 35 minutes.

MOLASSES RICE PUDDING

To serve 2 or 3:	To serve 4 to 6:	
AMOUNT	AMOUNT	INGREDIENTS
3/4 cup	1 1/2 cups	Cooked rice
1/4 cup	1/2 cup	Raisins
Dash	1/8 teaspoon	Salt
1	2	Eggs
1 1/4 cups	2 1/2 cups	Milk
2 tablespoons	1/4 cup	Unsulphured molasses
1 1/2 teaspoons	1 tablespoon	Butter
2 tablespoons	2 tablespoons	Sugar
1/4 teaspoon	1/4 teaspoon	Cinnamon

Combine rice and raisins in a casserole; sprinkle with salt. Beat together eggs and milk; blend in molasses. Stir into rice mixture; dot with butter. Combine sugar and cinnamon and sprinkle evenly over top. Bake in a 350°F. oven for 30 minutes. If desired, this mixture may be baked in individual custard cups.

WALNUT LINZER BALLS

To make 3 dozen balls:

AMOUNT	INGREDIENTS
1 1/2 cups	**Walnuts**
1/2 cup	**Butter**
1/2 cup	**Sugar**
1	**Egg, separated**
3/4 teaspoon	**Grated lemon peel**
1 cup	**Sifted all-purpose flour**
1/4 teaspoon	**Salt**
1/4 teaspoon	**Cinnamon**
1/8 teaspoon	**Ground cloves**
1/2 cup	**Apricot jam**

Grate 1 cup walnuts, using a Mouli grater, or put ⅝ cup at a time into blender, and blend very fine. Chop remaining ½ cup walnuts fine. Cream butter, sugar, egg yolk, and lemon peel together. Resift flour with salt, cinnamon, and ground cloves. Blend into creamed mixture. Add grated walnuts and mix well. Chill dough for 30 minutes or longer, for easier handling at this point. Shape into small balls. Beat egg white lightly. Dip balls in egg white, then roll in chopped walnuts. Place on greased baking sheet, and make an indentation in top of each. Fill indentations wtih jam. Bake at 350° F. for 18 minutes. Cool before storing.

BUTTERSCOTCH PICNIC BARS

To make 50 bars:

AMOUNT	INGREDIENTS
2/3 cup	**Butter**
2 1/4 cups	**Brown sugar, firmly packed**
3	**Eggs**
2 2/3 cups	**Sifted all-purpose flour**
2 1/2 teaspoons	**Baking powder**
1 teaspoon	**Salt**
1 cup	**Butterscotch-flavored morsels**
1 cup	**Chopped nuts**

Melt butter in a saucepan. Stir in brown sugar; remove from heat and cool for 10 minutes. Add eggs; beat until smooth. Sift together flour, baking powder and salt; stir into butter mixture. Add butterscotch morsels and nuts; mix well. Spread evenly in greased pan (15" x 10" x 1"). Bake in 350° F. oven about 25 minutes. Cool. Cut in 2-inch by 1½-inch bars.

WALNUT JUMBLE COOKIES

To make 30 cookies:

AMOUNT	INGREDIENTS
1/2 cup	Soft butter
1 cup	Brown sugar
1	Egg
1/2 cup	Dairy sour cream
1 teaspoon	Vanilla
1 3/4 cups	Sifted all-purpose flour
3/4 teaspoon	Baking soda
3/4 teaspoon	Salt
1 cup	Chopped walnuts

Beat butter and brown sugar together. Add egg, sour cream, and vanilla; beat until smooth. Resift flour with baking soda and salt; stir into batter. Beat with mixer, or vigorously by hand for 3 minutes. Add walnuts. Drop by tablespoonfuls onto a lightly greased baking sheet. Bake at 375° F. for 10 to 12 minutes. Cool before storing.

CHOCOLATE WALNUT DATE BARS

To make 18 bars:

AMOUNT	INGREDIENTS
2	Eggs
3/4 cup	Brown sugar
2 tablespoons	Soft butter
1 teaspoon	Vanilla
1 (1-ounce) square	Unsweetened chocolate, melted
1 cup	Chopped walnuts

AMOUNT	INGREDIENTS
1 cup	**Sliced pitted dates**
2/3 cup	**Sifted all-purpose flour**
1/2 teaspoon	**Baking powder**
1/4 teaspoon	**Salt**

Beat eggs, then beat in sugar, butter, and vanilla until well blended. Stir in melted chocolate, walnuts, and sliced dates. Resift flour with baking powder and salt; stir this into first mixture. Turn into greased 9-inch-square pan. Bake at 325°F. for 25 to 30 minutes. Cool, the cut into bars about 1½ inches by 3 inches.

PEANUT BUTTER–GINGERBREAD SQUARES

To make 15 squares:

AMOUNT	INGREDIENTS
1/2 cup	**Butter**
1/2 cup	**Peanut butter**
1/2 cup	**Sugar**
1/2 cup	**Unsulphured molasses**
1	**Egg**
1 1/2 cups	**Sifted all-purpose flour**
1/2 teaspoon	**Salt**
1 1/2 teaspoons	**Baking powder**
1/2 teaspoon	**Baking soda**
1 teaspoon	**Cinnamon**
1/2 teaspoon	**Ground cloves**
1/2 cup	**Hot water**

Cream together butter, peanut butter, and sugar. Blend in molasses and egg. Sift together flour, salt, baking powder, baking soda, cinnamon, and cloves. Stir into molasses mixture, alternating with the hot water. Turn into a greased pan (13″ x 9″ x 2″). Bake in 350° F. oven for 25 minutes. Cool. Cut into 2½-inch squares. Serve with a scoop of ice cream, if desired.

BROWNIE CUPCAKES

To make 18 cupcakes:

AMOUNT	INGREDIENTS
2 squares (1-ounce each)	Unsweetened chocolate
1/2 cup	Sugar
2	Eggs, separated
3/4 cup	Walnuts
1/3 cup	Soft butter
1 1/2 cups	Sifted powdered sugar (confectioners')
1 teaspoon	Vanilla
1 3/4 cups	Sifted all-purpose flour
3 teaspoons	Baking powder
1 teaspoon	Salt
2/3 cup	Milk

Melt chocolate; add sugar, stirring well. Beat in one egg yolk until mixture is smooth. Set aside. Chop walnuts. Beat butter, powdered sugar and vanilla together until creamy; beat in remaining egg yolk. Resift flour with baking powder and salt. Add to creamed mixture alternately with milk. Stir in chocolate mixture and walnuts. Beat egg whites stiff; fold into chocolate batter. Spoon into muffin pans lined with paper cupcake liners, filling about 2/3 full. Bake at 375° F. for 20 minutes. Cool before storing. Serve plain, or topped with sifted powdered sugar, or spread with Chocolate Butter Frosting (below). Garnish with walnut halves, if desired.

CHOCOLATE BUTTER FROSTING

To frost 18 cupcakes:

AMOUNT	INGREDIENTS
3 tablespoons	Soft butter
2 cups	Sifted powdered sugar (confectioners')
1/4 cup	Light cream or milk
2 squares (1-ounce each)	Unsweetened chocolate, melted

Beat butter, powdered sugar and light cream together until smooth. Blend in chocolate. Add a little more cream if necessary for good spreading consistency. Spread at once.

If you ever feel a yearning for an old-fashioned coffee cake, pop this one into the oven. The Orange Glaze topping makes it especially good —use it to top a store-bought sponge cake when you're in a hurry.

ORANGE OATMEAL COFFEE CAKE

Makes 9 servings:

AMOUNT	INGREDIENTS
1/2 cup (1 stick)	Butter
1 cup	Sugar
2	Eggs
1 1/2 cups	Sifted flour
2 teaspoons	Baking powder
1/2 teaspoon	Cinnamon
1/4 teaspoon	Salt
1 cup	Quick-cooking oatmeal, uncooked
1 cup	Milk

In a large mixing bowl, cream the butter; gradually add sugar and beat until light and fluffy. Beat in eggs one at a time. Sift together flour, baking powder, cinnamon, and salt; mix in oatmeal. Add to creamed mixture alternately with milk beginning and ending with dry ingredients. Turn into a buttered 8-inch-square pan. Bake in a preheated 350° F. oven for 35 to 45 minutes. While warm, spread with Orange Glaze (below). Place under broiler until topping is bubbly, about 2 minutes. Cool cake slightly in pan on wire rack before cutting.

ORANGE GLAZE

AMOUNT	INGREDIENTS
1/4 cup	Butter
1/2 cup	Light brown sugar, firmly packed
1/2 cup	Chopped nuts
3 tablespoons	Orange juice

In a small mixing bowl, cream the butter; stir in brown sugar, nuts, and juice. Spread over cake. Place under broiler until topping is bubbly, about 2 minutes. Serve warm.

Remember way back when you used to make mud pies? Bottoms-Up Apple Cake flips over much the same way—only this time there's something really good to eat. The cake itself is a simple one-egg recipe that's light and moist and easy to do.

BOTTOMS-UP APPLE CAKE

To serve 9:

AMOUNT	INGREDIENTS
2 tablespoons	Butter
1/2 cup	Light brown sugar, firmly packed
1/2 teaspoon	Cinnamon
2 cups	Peeled, thinly sliced cooking apples
2 cups	Sifted flour
1 cup	Sugar
2 1/2 teaspoons	Baking powder
1/2 teaspoon	Salt
1/2 cup (1 stick)	Butter, slightly softened
3/4 cup	Milk
1	Egg, beaten

In a 9-inch-square baking pan melt 2 tablespoons butter in oven; mix brown sugar and cinnamon; sprinkle over melted butter. Arrange sliced apple in rows in bottom of pan. Set aside. Into a large mixing bowl sift together flour, sugar, baking powder, and salt. Add ½ cup butter and ½ cup milk. Beat 2 minutes at medium speed of an electric mixer. Add remaining ¼ cup milk and egg; beat 2 additional minutes at medium speed. Spread batter over apples in pan. Bake in preheated 375° F. oven for 30 to 40 minutes. Cool in pan on wire rack for 10 minutes. Invert onto serving plate. Cut into squares. Delicious when served warm.

APPLE CRISP

To serve 2 or 3:	To serve 4 to 6:	
AMOUNT	AMOUNT	INGREDIENTS
2 cups	4 cups	Canned apple sauce
1 1/2 teaspoons	1 tablespoon	Lemon juice
1/4 teaspoon	1/2 teaspoon	Cinnamon
1/4 teaspoon	1/2 teaspoon	Nutmeg
2 tablespoons	1/4 cup	Melted butter
1/4 cup	1/2 cup	Sugar
2 tablespoons	1/4 cup	Orange juice
2 1/2 cups	5 cups	Corn flakes

Combine apple sauce, lemon juice, cinnamon, and nutmeg in a saucepan. Simmer for 10 minutes. Pour into a square baking pan. Combine melted butter, sugar, orange juice, and corn flakes. Sprinkle over the apple sauce. Bake in a 400° F. oven until topping begins to brown, about 15 minutes. Serve immediately. Top with cream, if desired.

When fresh peaches are in season, bake deceptively simple Peach Kuchen. It boasts ripe sweet sliced peaches plus a spice-seasoned buttery crumb crust dotted with raisins—and ever so good!

PEACH KUCHEN

To serve 9:

AMOUNT	INGREDIENTS
1/2 cup (1 stick)	Butter
1 cup	Sugar
1 1/2 cups	Sifted flour
1 teaspoon	Cinnamon
1/2 teaspoon	Baking powder
1/2 teaspoon	Salt
1/4 teaspoon	Nutmeg
3 cups	Sliced fresh peaches (about 5 medium)
1/4 cup	Raisins, cut up

In a small mixing bowl, cream butter until soft; add sugar and beat until light and fluffy. Sift together flour, cinnamon, baking powder, salt, and nutmeg; gradually add to creamed mixture. (Mixture will be crumbly.) Set aside 1 cup of mixture. Press remaining crumb mixture on bottom of an 8-inch-square baking pan and extend crumbs ½ inch up the sides of the pan. Combine ½ cup of remaining crumb mixture with peach slices; arrange peach mixture in the baking pan atop crumb shell. Combine raisins with remaining ½ cup crumb mixture; sprinkle on top of peaches. Bake in preheated 375° F. oven for 40 to 45 minutes. Cut in squares; serve hot or cool.

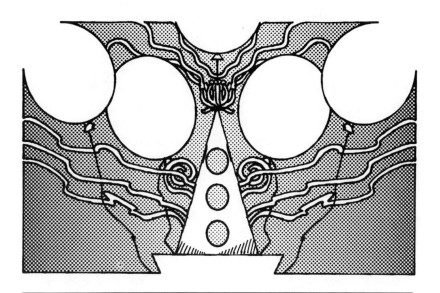

17 · Party Starters

No matter how informal an invitation is, people arrive hungry. That's a fact of life nobody ever tells you, but you learn fast after one such onslaught. It's best to have ready and waiting a few bowls filled with nibbles, and one or two bowls with dips or spreads surrounded with crackers that won't crumble.

Avoid spending hours making decorated hors d' oeuvres that will either dry out and curl up at the edges or get soggy and unappealing in the center. They'll probably be eaten in spite of it all, but it's a waste of time and your guests' appetites. Anyway, those platters are an embarrassment when they are half empty and scattered with limp offerings.

Instead, concentrate on preparing do-it-yourself pickup food, so your guests can wander around and keep busy fixing little snacks while chatting. Limit yourself to items that can be dipped, spread, sliced, or speared with a minimum of drip and a maximum of pleasure.

Don't forget to have plenty of small paper napkins available, and party picks if you need them. Set up a wastebasket or tray where these items may be disposed of, preventing a mess before it happens. Be sure to have extra Sterno or candles if you are using a non-electric chafing dish, and back yourself up with a reserve of peanuts, popcorn, or pretzels, in case you need more refills than you expected.

Many recipes in this book serve sizable numbers of people. They are excellent for company dinner or buffet service, if that is what you are planning to do. The recipes in this chapter are designed to get your party started—whether you are having a group in for drinks, for dinner, or for after-dinner socializing. Once you have prepared for the event, relax and enjoy yourself—nobody has fun with a hovering host!

NUTTY CHEESE BALL

To make 3 cups:

AMOUNT	INGREDIENTS
2 packages (3-ounces each)	Chive cream cheese
1 package (8-ounce)	Cream cheese
1 can (8 1/2-ounce)	Crushed pineapple, well drained
2 cups	Chopped pecans
1/4 cup	Chopped green pepper
2 tablespoons	Grated onion
1/2 teaspoon	Seasoned salt

Soften chive and cream cheese and mash together. Stir in pineapple, 1 cup of the chopped pecans, and the green pepper, grated onion, and seasoned salt. Chill well, then form into a ball; roll ball in remaining cup of chopped pecans. To garnish, top with a sprig of fluffy parsley. Serve with crackers for easy spreading.

NOTE: If there is any leftover cheese, form into a new ball, roll it in chopped pecans, and it's ready to serve again.

A flavorful cheese spread, that keeps well and mellows as it stands, makes unexpected guests easier to entertain. This one is made of three kinds of cheeses, blended together with wine for a piquant taste.

THREE-CHEESE SPREAD

To make 2 cups of cheese spread:

AMOUNT	INGREDIENTS
1 cup	Cheddar cheese spread
1 package (8-ounce)	Cream cheese
1/4 cup	Blue cheese
1/2 teaspoon	Curry powder
1 teaspoon	Dry mustard
1/3 cup	Chablis or dry sherry wine

Combine three cheeses until smooth. Add curry powder, dry mustard, and wine. When smooth, turn into a storing container; cover and refrigerate for at least 24 hours. Serve with crispy crackers.

CHIVE CHEESE ALMOND DIP

AMOUNT	INGREDIENTS
6 ounces	Chive cream cheese
1/4 cup	Milk
1/4 teaspoon	Salt
1 teaspoon	Prepared mustard
1/2 cup	Chopped toasted almonds
2 cups	Corn chips

Soften cheese with milk. Add salt, mustard, and almonds. Fill a small bowl with this mixture and chill until serving time. Serve surrounded with corn chips for dipping.

AVOCADO DIP

AMOUNT	INGREDIENTS
2	Very ripe avocados
2 drops	Tabasco sauce
1/2 teaspoon	Salt
2 teaspoons	Lemon juice
2 tablespoons	White horseradish
1/2 cup	Dairy sour cream

Mash avocados. Add Tabasco sauce. Stir in salt, lemon juice, horseradish, sour cream. Mix well and chill for at least 1 hour. Serve with pretzels, fresh vegetables, and fresh fruit slices as dippers.

DILL DIP

AMOUNT	INGREDIENTS
1 1/2 cups	Mayonnaise
1/2 cup	Dairy sour cream
3 tablespoons	Finely chopped fresh dill
1/4 teaspoon	Grated onion
2 teaspoons	Chopped chives

Combine mayonnaise and sour cream; add fresh dill (if you must substitute, use 1 teaspoon dried dill). Add onion and chives; mix well and chill. Serve with plenty of salty pretzels.

MUSTARD DIP

AMOUNT	INGREDIENTS
1/2 cup	Prepared mustard
2 tablespoons	Salad oil
2 tablespoons	Wine vinegar
1/2 cup	Mayonnaise
1 teaspoon	Chopped chives

Stir all ingredients together until well blended. Refrigerate for several hours or overnight. Serve with pretzels.

SHRIMP PÂTÉ

To make 1 cup:	*To make 2 cups:*	
AMOUNT	AMOUNT	INGREDIENTS
1 1/2 cups	3 cups	Cooked fresh or canned shrimp
1/4 cup	1/2 cup	White dinner wine
1/4 teaspoon	1/2 teaspoon	Dry mustard
1/8 teaspoon	1/4 teaspoon	Dried dill
Dash	Dash or two	Tabasco sauce
1/4 cup	1/2 cup	Soft butter

Mash shrimp fine with wine and seasonings, or blend smooth in an electric blender. Beat in soft butter until well mixed. Pack into small crock or mold. Cover and refrigerate overnight to mellow and blend flavors. Serve with crisp salted crackers.

Fondue is a friendly ice-breaker for a large party. Each guest spears a cube of bread from the soft side through the crust, then dips into the pot with a swirling motion. Remember to keep the fondue stirred as it bubbles over medium heat—if it gets too hot it will become stringy; too cold, it will toughen.

SWISS FONDUE

To serve 10 to 12 as an appetizer:

AMOUNT	INGREDIENTS:
1 clove	Garlic
1 1/2 tablespoons	Cornstarch
1/3 cup	Kirsch
1 1/2 cups	Dry white wine
1 1/2 pounds	Swiss cheese, grated
1/4 teaspoon	Baking soda
Dash each of	White pepper, paprika, nutmeg

Rub inside of fondue pot well with cut side of garlic, then discard garlic. Mix cornstarch and Kirsch, set aside. Put wine into fondue pot and heat until bubbles start to rise to the surface. Add cheese by thirds, stirring constantly until all cheese is melted. When mixture starts to bubble, quickly add cornstarch mixture, stirring constantly until thickened. Add baking soda, pepper, paprika, and nutmeg, mixing well. Stir occasionally. If the fondue becomes too thick while serving, gradually add heated wine while stirring briskly.

FONDUE DOFINO

To serve 4 to 6:

AMOUNT	INGREDIENTS
1 clove	Garlic
1 bottle (12-ounce)	Beer
1 pound	Dofino cheese
2 tablespoons	Flour
2 teaspoons	Prepared mustard
1/4 teaspoon	Salt
1/8 teaspoon	Pepper
1	French bread, cut into cubes

Rub fondue pot with cut garlic clove; discard garlic. Place over low heat and pour in beer; heat to bubbling. Cut cheese into slivers and toss with flour and mustard; add to beer, a handful at a time, stirring over low heat until mixture is creamy and smooth. Add salt and pepper. Keep warm, stirring occasionally, and serve with bread cubes and long forks for spearing.

SHRIMP QUICHE

To serve 8 to 10 as an appetizer (or 6 as a main course):

AMOUNT	INGREDIENTS
1 pound	Shrimp (fresh or frozen)
1/4 pound	Swiss cheese, grated
1 package (6-ounce)	Grated Gruyère cheese
3	Eggs
1 cup	Light cream
1 tablespoon	Flour
1/4 teaspoon	Salt
Dash	Pepper
1/4 teaspoon	Dry mustard

To serve 8 to 10 as an appetizer (or 6 as a main course):

AMOUNT	INGREDIENTS
1/2 teaspoon	Worcestershire sauce
Dash	Tabasco sauce
9-inch	Unbaked pastry shell (available at your grocer's freezer counter)

Clean and devein shrimp; cut in small pieces. Combine Swiss and Gruyère cheeses; set aside. Combine eggs, cream, flour, salt, pepper, mustard, Worcestershire and Tabasco sauces. Spread ¾ of cheese mixture in pastry shell. Add shrimp and cover with remaining cheese. Pour egg mixture over cheese and shrimp. Bake in a 400°F. oven for 15 minutes; reduce heat to 325°F. and continue baking for 40 minutes, or until knife inserted in center comes out clean. Let stand for 10 minutes before serving. Serve warm. (Can be refrigerated and reheated just before serving time.)

MEATBALLS IN RED WINE SAUCE

To serve 6: AMOUNT	*To serve 12:* AMOUNT	INGREDIENTS
1 small	1 large	Finely chopped onion
1/2 cup	1 cup	Fine bread crumbs
1 pound	2 pounds	Ground beef
1	2	Eggs
1/4 teaspoon	1/2 teaspoon	Salt
1/8 teaspoon	1/4 teaspoon	Pepper
1/4 teaspoon	1/2 teaspoon	Curry powder
2 tablespoons	1/4 cup	Grated Parmesan cheese
1/4 teaspoon	1/2 teaspoon	Worcestershire sauce
1	2	Garlic cloves, diced
1/2 cup	1 cup	Flour
1 tablespoon	2 tablespoons	Salad oil
1/2 cup	1 cup	Red table wine
1/4 cup	1/2 cup	Beef consommé
1 can (8-ounce)	2 cans	Tomato sauce
1/8 teaspoon	1/4 teaspoon	Oregano

Combine onion, bread crumbs, beef, eggs, salt, pepper, curry powder, Parmesan cheese, and Worcestershire sauce. Form into 1½-inch meatballs. Roll each lighly in flour. Place salad oil and diced garlic in a large skillet; add meatballs and brown on all sides for about 8 minutes. Meanwhile, combine wine, consommé, tomato sauce, and oregano in a large saucepan and bring to a simmering point. Add meatballs and simmer together for about 25 minutes. Serve with toothpicks in a chafing dish, or on spaghetti or rice as a main course.

You'll never be at a loss for an unexpected late snack if you keep frozen waffles in your freezer compartment, Swiss cheese in your refrigerator, and cans of sauerkraut and corned beef in your cupboard. Within minutes, you can produce Waffles Reuben for eight.

WAFFLES REUBEN

To serve 8:

AMOUNT	INGREDIENTS
1 package (12-ounce)	Frozen round waffles
1 can (1-pound)	Sauerkraut
1 1/8 teaspoon	Caraway seed
1 can (12-ounce)	Corned beef
1 tablespoon	Prepared mustard
1 package (8-ounce)	Swiss cheese slices

Preheat broiler. Heat waffles according to package directions. Heat sauerkraut with caraway seed and drain. Cut corned beef in 8 slices. Top each wafflle with a corned beef slice. Spread beef with mustard. Spoon on hot sauerkraut. Top with cheese. Broil 4 inches from source of heat for about 2 minutes, or until cheese is bubbly and lightly browned. Serve at once.

BACON 'N' TOMATO RAREBIT

To serve 6:

AMOUNT	INGREDIENTS
6 slices	Bacon
1/2 cup	Chopped onions
1/2 cup	Chopped green peppers
1/4 cup	Flour
1 cup	Milk
1 can (8-ounce)	Tomato sauce
1 cup (1/4 pound)	Shredded sharp Cheddar cheese
1 teaspoon	Worcestershire sauce
6	English muffins, split and toasted

Cook bacon until crisp; drain. Cook onion and green pepper in the bacon fat until tender. Blend in flour. Stir in milk and tomato sauce, mix until smooth; cook until thickened. Add cheese and Worcestershire sauce. Stir until cheese is melted. Serve over toasted English muffins. Top each serving with a strip of cooked bacon.

CHOCOLATE FUDGE

To make 2 pounds of fudge:

AMOUNT	INGREDIENTS
1 jar (10-ounce)	Marshmallow cream
2/3 cup	Evaporated milk
1/4 cup	Butter
1 1/2 cups	Sugar
1/4 teaspoon	Salt
1 package (12-ounce)	Semi-sweet chocolate morsels
1 teaspoon	Vanilla
1 cup	Chopped nuts

Combine marshmallow cream, evaporated milk, butter, sugar, and salt in a saucepan. Place over moderate heat; stir constantly until mixture comes to a full rolling boil. Boil 5 minutes, continuing to stir constantly. Remove from heat. Add chocolate morsels and vanilla; stir until smooth. Stir in nuts. Turn into a greased 9-inch-square pan. Chill until firm. Cut into squares.

PUDDING BRITTLE

To make 8 cups of candy:

AMOUNT	INGREDIENTS
1 tablespoon	Butter
3 tablespoons	Light corn syrup
1 package (3-ounce)	Butterscotch pudding mix (cooking type)
3 cups	Rice Krispies cereal
1/2 cup	Coarsely chopped salted cocktail peanuts

Measure butter and syrup into a saucepan. Cook over moderate heat until butter is melted, stirring occasionally. Stir in pudding mix; bring to full boil, stirring constantly. Continue cooking for 1 minute, stirring constantly. Remove from heat. Add cereal and peanuts to cooked pudding mixture; mix thoroughly. Spread in thin layer on waxed paper or buttered baking sheet; cool. Break into small pieces to serve as candy. Store in tightly covered container.

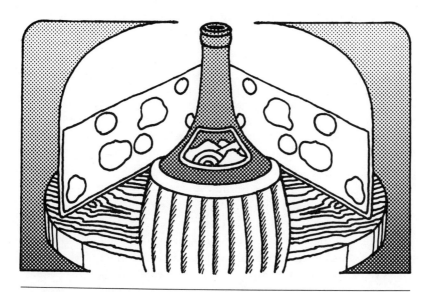

18 · Wine and Cheese Savoir Faire

Sooner or later you will be faced with decisions about what wine or cheese to buy for a particular occasion. There is always the searching moment when you try to remember whether to serve them chilled or at room temperature, and what goes with what. Ultimately, your own good sense of taste will decide these things for you, but until you have sure footing, here is some helpful information to guide you in your purchases.

ABOUT WINE

Rules are meant to be broken when it comes to wine, but it is helpful to know what the rules are before you choose to go your own way. A simple way to remember what wine goes with what: Serve red wine with red meat and white wine with fish and fowl. Uncork red wine about an hour before serving to let it "breathe" at room temperature. No need to chill it unless this is your preference.

White wine should be chilled for several hours before serving and is uncorked at serving time. Of course, a happy medium is to choose a chilled pink wine known as "rosé," but hopefully you will choose it because you really like the taste, rather than as a copout in a wine-food situation.

Basically, the more highly seasoned the food, the more robust should be the flavor of the wine that goes with it. In choosing a red wine you would take into consideration the kind of meat you are serving.

For example, Chianti (an Italian-born wine that is also produced in California) is a full-bodied yet mellow wine which goes well with the highly spiced Italian sauces. But such a wine would overcome the subtler flavors of roast leg of lamb—so a better selection for that would be a claret, such as Cabernet Sauvignon or Zinfandel. Either of these is an excellent compliment to the flavors of lamb or roast beef with natural gravy. Steak au Poivre, on the other hand, requires a more robust, more sturdy wine, such as a Burgundy.

Even among the white wines, there are light ones and full-bodied ones. A very light dish, such as simple broiled scallops, would be best accompanied by a light, flowery Rhine wine such as a Riesling. To indicate the difference, another scallop dish, Coquilles St. Jacques, with a rich cream sauce, goes beautifully with the fuller-bodied Chablis wine, such as Pinot Chardonnay.

Rosé wine is so versatile that it is the perfect wine to take along on a picnic. It need not be as icy cold as a white wine, which solves the problem of transporting it and the hot weather warming it up a bit during the meal. It goes well with all foods, though because of its lighter body it matches best with light meats, foul, fish, and all kinds of sandwiches and salads.

Of course, there are other classes of wines besides these table wines, so to give you a broader scope of what is available and when to use it, let's break them down into four classifications:

APPETIZER WINES: These are usually dry (meaning without a sweet taste but not sour) and are served before meals or with the soup course. Chill them or serve at room temperature, or pour over ice:

Sherry (dry to sweet)

Vermouth (dry to sweet)

Special Natural Wines (flavored with fruit juices, mint, coffee, herbs, and other essences)

DINNER WINES: Most people prefer red table wine served at room temperature with steaks, roasts, game, spaghetti, cheeses, stews, casseroles. Rosé wine is preferred when it is chilled, with ham, pork, veal, lamb, and poultry. White table wine is preferred chilled by most people, and is served with fish, shellfish, and poultry:

Red Table Wines   *Burgundy* (dry)
                                  Claret (dry)
                                  Red Chianti (dry)
                                  Vino Rosso (semi-sweet or mellow red)
                                  Concord (sweet)
                                  Rosé (pink)

White Table Wines   *Chablis* (dry)
                                  Rhine Wine (dry)
                                  Sauterne (dry to sweet)
                                  White Chianti (dry)
                                  Light Muscat (dry to sweet)
                                  Catawba (dry to semi-sweet)
                                  Delaware (dry)

SWEET DESSERT WINES: These are served after dinner, either with dessert or later. They are all sweet, rich wines that are particularly good with fruit, nuts, cheese, plain cake, cookies. Serve at room temperature:

     Port (red, white, or tawny)
     Tokay
     Muscatel (gold, red, black)
     Angelica
     Madeira
     Marsala
     Sweet or *Cream Sherry*

SPARKLING WINES: These are appropriate at any time, along with food or alone. Serve them thoroughly chilled:

Champagne (gold or pink)
    Brut (very dry)
    Sec (semi-dry)
    Doux (sweet)
Sparkling Burgundy
Sparkling Muscat (sweet)
Sparkling Rosé (dry to semi-sweet)

California wines are usually identified by the main grape variety from which they are made, whereas European wines are named after the district in which it is grown. If you are interested in the origin of the more popular imported table wines, here is a list that will help you to identify them:

RED TABLE WINES	ORIGIN	TASTE
Bardolino	Verona, Italy	Dry
Beaujolais	Burgundy, France	Dry
Bordeaux Rouge	Bordeaux, France	Dry
Chambertin	Burgundy, France	Dry
Châteauneuf-du-Pape	Rhône, France	Dry
Chianti	Tuscany, Italy	Dry
Grignolino	Piedmont, Italy	Dry
Pommard	Burgundy, France	Dry
Rioja	Spain	Dry
Valpolicella	Veneto, Italy	Dry

ROSÉ TABLE WINE		
Rosé	France, Portugal	Dry

WHITE TABLE WINES		
Bernkasteler	Moselle, Germany	Dry
Bordeaux Blanc	Bordeaux, France	Medium Dry
Chablis	Burgundy, France	Dry
Château d'Yquem	Bordeaux, France	Sweet
Chianti	Tuscany, Italy	Dry
Graves	Bordeaux, France	Medium Dry
Liebfraumilch	Rhine, Germany	Dry
Meursault	Burgundy, France	Dry
Montrachet	Burgundy, France	Dry
Moselblumchen	Moselle, Germany	Dry

Niersteiner	Rhine, Germany	Dry
Piesporter	Moselle, Germany	Dry
Pouilly Fuissé	Burgundy, France	Dry
Riesling	Rhine, Germany	Dry
Sauternes	Bordeaux, France	Sweet
Soave	Veneto, Italy	Dry
Traminer	Alsace, France	Dry
Vouvray	Touraine, France	Medium Dry

NOTE: The word "dry" always refers to the absence or near-absence of sweetness. It is not sour, it is simply not sweet.

Store wine away from the light, preferably in a cool place. Lay corked bottles on their sides to keep the corks moist and tight. If the bottles have screw caps, they can be safely stored in an upright position.

Traditionally, wine is served in clear, stemmed glasses. Fill them about halfway, leaving room for the aroma to gather above the wine. A tulip-shaped glass is suitable for any kind of wine, so choose this shape for your first wine glasses.

ABOUT WINE AND CHEESE TOGETHER

Here again, the rule of matching strength of flavors applies. Thus, you would scarcely serve a delicate Riesling with a sharp Roquefort —better with a really rich, full Burgundy, Pinot Noir, or Chianti. A fine aged Brie can easily go with the fuller-bodied white wines, such as Pinot Chardonnay and Chablis, as well as the lighter reds— Gamay Beaujolais, Claret, Cabernet Sauvignon and Zinfandel. Any of the flavored, mild, and slightly sweeter cheeses should be served with light wines—preferably Rhine wines, or the sweeter white table wines such as Semillon and Sauvignon Blanc.

Here are some good wine-cheese combinations to try:

CHEESE	WINE
Mild Cheddar (American)	Zinfandel, Gamay, Chablis, rosé.
Sharp Cheddar	Pinot Noir, Burgundy, Chianti
Roquefort	Pinot Noir, Burgundy, Chianti

Monterey Jack	Zinfandel, claret, Chablis,
	Pinot Chardonnay
Port du Salut	Zinfandel, claret, Rhine
Tilsit	Zinfandel, claret, Burgundy, Rhine
Swiss	Riesling, Rhine
Neufchatel	Riesling, Rhine

ABOUT CHEESE

When you are on your own, you suddenly become adventurous about tasting food that is different from what you have always been served at home. While you are seeking out new taste experiences, explore the world of cheese—for cheese is synonymous with versatility and good nutrition, and is available in some form that pleases almost every palate.

It helps to know the different ripening classifications of cheese, what they taste like in a general way, and how best to use them after you have made your purchase. The following information will aid you in your selections:

SOFT, UNRIPENED VARIETIES OF NATURAL CHEESES: These are consumed fresh, soon after manufacture, as they contain a relatively high moisture content and do not undergo any curing or ripening.

KIND	CHARACTERISTICS	USES
Cottage, plain, or creamed	Mild, slightly acid flavor, soft curd particles, white to creamy white	Appetizers, salads, some cakes, dips
Cream	Delicate, slightly acid flavor, soft, smooth in texture, white	Salads, dips, sandwiches, snacks, cake, desserts
Neufchatel	Mild acid flavor, soft and smooth like cream cheese but lower in milkfat, white	Salads, dips, sandwiches, snacks, cake, desserts
Ricotta	Mild sweet nutlike flavor, soft, moist texture, or dry and suitable for grating, white	Salads, lasagne, ravioli, other main dishes, desserts

FIRM, UNRIPENED VARIETIES OF NATURAL CHEESES: These are also consumed while fresh but because of the low moisture content may be kept for several weeks or months.

KIND	CHARACTERISTICS	USES
Gjetost	Sweetish, caramel flavor, firm buttery consistency, golden brown	Desserts, snacks
Mysost	Sweetish, caramel flavor, firm buttery consistency, light brown	Desserts, snacks
Mozzarella	Delicate mild flavor, slightly firm, plastic texture, creamy white	Main dishes, as pizza and lasagne, sandwiches, snacks

SOFT, RIPENED VARIETIES OF NATURAL CHEESES: In these cheeses the curing progresses from the outside to the center, and curing continues as long as the temperature is favorable. These cheeses contain more moisture than the semi-soft ripened varieties, and therefore have a softer creamier texture.

KIND	CHARACTERISTICS	USES
Brie	Mild to pungent flavor, soft smooth texture, creamy yellow interior, edible thin brown and white crust	Appetizers, sandwiches, desserts, snacks
Camembert	Mild to tangy flavor, soft smooth texture, runny when ripened, creamy yellow interior, edible thin white or gray-white crust	Appetizers, desserts, snacks
Limburger	Highly pungent, very strong flavor, soft smooth texture, creamy white interior, reddish-yellow surface	Appetizers, desserts, snacks

SEMISOFT, RIPENED VARIETIES OF NATURAL CHEESES: These ripen from the center as well as from the surface of the cheese. Curing continues as long as the temperature is favorable. These cheeses contain a higher moisture content than the firm, ripened cheeses, but a lower moisture content than the soft ripened cheeses.

KIND	CHARACTERISTICS	USES
Bel Paese	**Mild sweet flavor, light creamy yellow interior, slate gray surface, soft to medium-firm creamy texture**	Appetizers, sandwiches, desserts, snacks
Brick	**Mild to moderately sharp flavor, semisoft to medium-firm elastic texture, creamy white-to-yellow interior, brownish exterior**	Appetizers, sandwiches, desserts, snacks
Muenster	**Mild to mellow flavor, semisoft texture with many small openings, creamy white interior, yellowish-tan surface**	Appetizers, sandwiches, desserts, snacks
Port du Salut	**Mellow to robust flavor that is similar to Gouda, semisoft smooth elastic texture, creamy white or yellow**	Appetizers, desserts, snacks

FIRM, RIPENED VARIETIES OF NATURAL CHEESES: These cheeses ripen throughout the entire cheese, continuing as long as the temperature is favorable. They are lower in moisture content than the softer varieties and usually require a longer curing time.

KIND	CHARACTERISTICS	USES
Cheddar	**Mild to very sharp flavor, smooth texture, firm to crumbly, light cream to orange color**	Appetizers, main dishes, sauces, soups, sandwiches, salads, snacks
Colby	**Mild to mellow flavor similar to Cheddar, softer body and more open texture, light cream to orange color**	Sandwiches, snacks
Caciocavallo	**Slightly salty flavor, smooth and very firm texture, light or white interior, clay or tan-colored surface**	Snacks, desserts. Can be used for grating and cooking when fully cured

KIND	CHARACTERISTICS	USES
Edam	Mellow nutlike flavor, firm rubbery texture, creamy yellow interior, surface coated with red wax, usually shaped like a flat ball	Appetizers, salads, sandwiches, sauces, desserts, snacks
Gouda	Mellow nutlike and somewhat acid flavor, semisoft to firm smooth texture, often containing small holes, creamy yellow interior, usually has red waxcoating and is shaped like a flattened ball	Appetizers, salads, sauces, sandwiches, desserts, snacks
Provolone	Mellow to sharp flavor, smoky and salty, firm smooth texture, light creamy yellow, light brown, or golden yellow surface	Appetizers, sandwiches, desserts, snacks
Swiss	Mild sweet nutlike flavor, firm and smooth elastic body with large round holes, light yellow color	Sandwiches, salads, snacks

VERY HARD, RIPENED VARIETIES OF NATURAL CHEESES: These have a very slow rate of curing because of a very low moisture and very high salt content. They are mostly used for grating to flavor soups and main dishes, and may be purchased in grated form.

KIND	CHARACTERISTICS	USES
Parmesan	Sharp distinctive flavor, very hard granular texture, yellowish-white color	Grated for seasoning
Romano	Very sharp flavor, very hard granular texture, yellowish-white interior, greenish-black surface	Seasoning and table use, when hard, used for grating
Sap Sago	Sharp pungent cloverlike flavor, very hard texture suitable for grating; light green or sage green	Grated for seasoning

BLUE-VEIN MOLD, RIPENED VARIETIES OF NATURAL CHEESES: In these cheeses, as in the others, curing is accomplished by the aid of bacteria. These have the addition of a mold culture that grows throughout the interior of the cheese giving them characteristic flavor.

KIND	CHARACTERISTICS	USES
Blue (or Bleu)	Tangy flavor, semisoft crumbly texture, white interior marbled with blue veins of mold	Appetizers, salads, dressings, desserts, snacks
Gorgonzola	Tangy rich spicy flavor, semisoft and sometimes crumbly texture, creamy white interior, streaked with green veins of mold; clay-colored surface	Appetizers, salads, desserts, snacks
Roquefort	Sharp peppery piquant flavor, semisoft and sometimes crumbly texture, white interior streaked with blue-green veins of mold	Appetizers, salads, dressing, desserts, snacks
Stilton	Mild piquant flavor, open flaky texture, creamy-white interior streaked with blue-green veins of mold, wrinkled melon-like rind	Appetizers, salads, desserts, snacks

Cheese keeps best in the refrigerator, protected from drying out by an overwrapping of plastic wrap or aluminum foil. Soft cheeses such as cottage, cream, and Neufchatel are highly perishable, while hard cheeses such as Cheddar and Swiss keep for several months if free from mold. If any surface mold appears on hard cheese, trim it off before the cheese is used; unlike blue cheese mold that is part of the cheese and can be eaten, mold that penetrates cheese not ripened by molds should be cut away and discarded.

If your cheese has hardened and dried out, grate it and store it in the refrigerator in a tightly covered jar. Use it to season soups, salads, and main dishes.

When you serve several kinds of cheeses with crackers and fruit as a snack or dessert tray, select them from different categories so there will be a variety of textures and tastes. Apples and pears go well with blue or Roquefort cheeses; Tokay grapes with brick cheese; Camembert with apples, pears, and tart plums; Cheddar with tart apples or melon slices; Edam or Gouda with apples, orange sections, or pineapple spears; Muenster or Swiss with apples, seedless grapes, or orange sections; and Provolone with sweet Bartlett pears. Dip cut surfaces of apples and pears in lemon juice to prevent them from darkening and becoming unpleasant-looking.

Serve all but the soft cheeses at room temperature, removing them from the refrigerator at least one hour before to bring out the characteristic flavor and texture.

When cooking with cheese, keep the heat low; high temperatures and too-long cooking can make cheese tough and cause the fat to separate. It can also cause a loss of fine flavor. To prevent cheese toppings from drying out during baking, cover them with crumbs, or else add the cheese just minutes before removing the food from the oven.

If you want to add cheese to a sauce, shred it or dice it first so that it will melt quickly and easily. Add shredded cheese to an omelet just before folding it—after it is cooked, for best results. For broiled cheese sandwiches, heat only long enough for the cheese to melt and then serve at once.

While the selection of cheeses is a personal choice, there is a wide degree of tastes and textures to merit your attention. Do investigate their potential and you will be rewarded with many happy hours of pleasant repast.

Index of Recipes